ALLEGHENY NATIONAL FOREST HIKING GUIDE

Third Edition

By
Bruce Sundqu
Carolyn Weilacher ɪartz
and Jack Richardson

with the cooperation of the
Allegheny National Forest Staff
and Numerous Hikers

Published by:

Allegheny Group, Sierra Club
P.O. Box 8241
Pittsburgh, PA 15217

photolithoprinted by

EDWARDS
BROTHERS
INCORPORATED
800 EDWARDS DRIVE/P.O. BOX 1027/LILLINGTON, N.C. 27546

ALLEGHENY

NATIONAL FOREST

HIKING GUIDE

Third Edition

Printed in the United States of America

Copyright © 1990 by

Allegheny Group, Sierra Club

Front Cover:
Hiking along the Tanbark Trail just north of Hickory Creek Wilderness Area and west of Heart's Content Campground and Scenic Area. Lush fern fields and huge mossy boulders are typical scenery over much of Allegheny National Forest.

TABLE OF CONTENTS

No Substitute for Good Judgement

This guide has been compiled as an aid to those who want to take advantage of the outstanding opportunities for hiking, backpacking and ski-touring that the Allegheny National Forest has to offer. Though most trails are well-marked, staying on the trail still requires a reasonable degree of alertness in many areas. This guide should in no way be considered as a substitute for this alertness. The reader should be constantly aware of the possibility of errors in this guide and act accordingly. Off-trail hiking offers a great deal by way of scenery and solitude. But nothing in this guide should be construed as implying that such hiking is without certain risks, or that all who read this guide are sufficiently knowledgeable and experienced as to be capable of undertaking these risks. Many streams on the ANF are clean. Others are not. Nothing in this guide should be construed as implying that a given stream is safe to drink from. Whenever there is any doubt, standard purification procedures should be employed. In the final analysis your health and safety depend entirely on your own common sense and good judgement. This guide should in no way be regarded as a substitute for these.

Acknowledgements

The editors wish to express their gratitude to the following contributors to the contents of this guide:

Karen and Ed Atwood	Jane Delhunty Weilacher
Nancy & Ted Grisez	Larry J. Yartz
Tom & Sharon Hiegel	Ellen Burke (Chapman Dam)
Barbara & Robert Ronksley	Bob Peppel (" ")
Margaret Millward Blood	Dave Progar (" ")
Shirley Butts	Lynn Carnahan (USFS)
Quimby Mamula	Scott Dutchess (USFS)
Helen McGinnis	Mark Goebl (USFS)
Helen Marquard	Bill Hilyer (USFS)
Bobbie Moyers	Mary Hosmer (USFS)
Kessel Richardson	Terry Steffen (USFS)
John Warren	Jeff Stevenson (USFS)
Althea Weilacher	Ava Turnquist (USFS)
Derrell L. Weilacher	Dan Zimmerman (USFS)

Pennsylvania State Snowmobile Association

Numerous others contributed to the contents of the previous editions. Numerous others on the Allegheny National Forest staff have done an outstanding job at building and maintaining the trails described in this guide.

> Bruce Sundquist,
> Carolyn Weilacher Yartz
> Jack Richardson

Previous Editions:
Edition 1 August, 1977 (edited by Richard Pratt, Bruce Sundquist, Peter Wray)

Edition 2 May, 1982 (same editors as for Edition 1)

INTRODUCTION TO ALLEGHENY NATIONAL FOREST

> "To explore, enjoy and preserve the
> nation's forests, waters, wildlife,
> and wilderness........" Sierra Club

Being within an easy day's drive of urban centers such as
Buffalo, Cleveland, Pittsburgh, Harrisburg and Youngstown, the
Allegheny National Forest attracts hundreds of thousands of
visitors annually. Many of these visitors have long known the
Forest as an excellent hunting area while others have enjoyed
camping and water sports in the Forest since the 1930's. However, it is only in relatively recent times that the opportunities for hiking, backpacking and ski-touring in the Forest have
been fully appreciated. With the rising interest in hiking in
the 1960's, the U. S. Forest Service developed a section of the
North Country Trail through the Forest as part of a National
Trail System. Completion of this trail section has been a
major stimulus to the use of the Forest by experienced hikers.
By 1982 the addition of side trails and the upgrading of some
old trails had extended the Forest trail system to 168 miles.
Today (1990) 226 miles of foot trails are found on the Allegheny National Forest. The purpose of this guide is to describe
these maintained trails, some informal trails, and some areas
in the Forest where off-trail foot travel may be pleasurably
pursued. Hopefully the user's knowledge and enjoyment of the
Forest, in all seasons, will be enhanced and lead to enlight-
ened public interest in the management of the Forest as a truly
national resource.

General Description of the Forest

The Allegheny National Forest consists of a single tract
of over 512,000 acres (800 square miles) in the four northwestern Pennsylvania counties of Elk, Forest, McKean and Warren.
It is one of 15 national forests in the eastern U.S. It is
roughly bounded on the west by the Allegheny River, on the
north by the New York state line, on the east by highway US
219, and on the south by PA 36 and the Clarion River. The Forest lies on the Allegheny Plateau, cut by creeks draining west
into the Allegheny River and south into the Clarion River as
shown in Map 1. In general, the more rugged terrain is to be
found in the western part of the Forest, while the higher elevations are found in the eastern part and the deepest snows are
found in the northern part, being closer to Lake Erie. Elevations range between 1100 and 2400 feet.

The original virgin forest was composed of mature stands
of northern hardwoods, with interspersed groves of white pine
and hemlock. Indian tribes hunted in the area and camped along
the Allegheny and Clarion Rivers with little disturbance of the

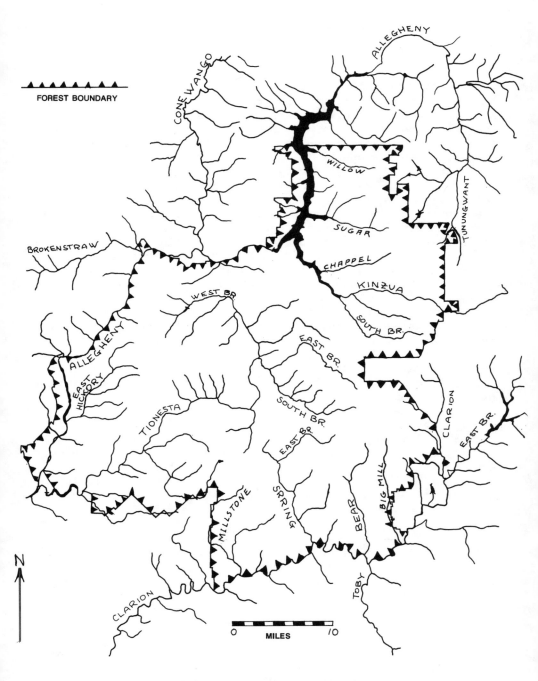

FOREST BOUNDARY

MAP 1 – PRINCIPAL WATERSHEDS OF THE ALLEGHENY NATIONAL FOREST

2

forest. In the nineteenth century, settlers moved into the region and began clearing a portion of the forest for farmland. The first intensive logging operations involved floating logs, including most of the white pine, down the Allegheny and Clarion Rivers. Towards the end of the last century, narrow-gauge railroads were built throughout the forest in order to remove the remaining trees, including the hemlocks for the tanning industry. By the early 1900s little of the virgin forest had survived the operations of the short-sighted timber companies. Fires burned repeatedly and much of the soil washed away. The public outrage was part of the reason that on September 24, 1923, the only National Forest in Pennsylvania was established. At that time the Forest consisted of little more than brush, so that today most of the trees are in the 65- to 75-year age class. The annual timber growth is estimated to be about 29 million cubic feet. The annual volume of suitable wood products harvested during recent years has been around 65 million board-feet (around 10 million cubic feet). The present-day visitor sees an evolving forest that, if allowed to succeed naturally, will be quite different in 20 years.

In today's forest the predominant tree species are the black cherry, red maple, sugar maple, oaks, birch and beech--in that order of abundance--with conifers, mostly hemlocks, concentrated in stream valleys. For a more complete listing of the common native trees to be found in the forest, see page 13. Black cherry logs are exported, mainly to Europe for furniture and veneer. Individual black cherry trees (and some oaks) can be worth several thousand dollars on the stump.

As with most other National Forests, the Allegheny National Forest is managed for several purposes. In addition to timber, the Forest yields oil, gas, and minerals. As early as 1860, northwestern Pennsylvania became the world's leading

KEY MAP

oil producing area. Many of the wells are now quiet, but about half the original oil and gas still lies beneath the Forest, and the Federal Government owns the oil, gas, and mineral rights for only six percent of the area. Much of the remaining land is open to entry by oil and gas drillers, whenever the economics are favorable. Oil, gas, and mineral issues are discussed on page 21.

The third major use of the Forest is recreation, including cabin vacations, boating, camping, hiking, fishing and hunting. The Forest Service estimates that, in 1989, use on all areas of the Forest was 2.4 million visitor-days (1.7 million visitor-days in 1988). Four beaches, six boat launches, 17 campgrounds, three scenic overlooks and nine picnic areas satisfy those who prefer developed facilities. Many recreation areas are near the Allegheny Reservoir, a 27-mile lake on the upper Allegheny River, impounded by Kinzua Dam. Six of the 10 campgrounds on the Allegheny Reservoir can be reached only by boat or on foot.

All of the above indicates that the Allegheny National Forest is a relatively "civilized" forest and indeed there are relatively few small areas where man's intrusion is not evident. For example, within the Forest are 503 miles of state highways, 263 miles of township roads, and 535 miles of roads maintained by the Forest Service. There are also numerous inholdings throughout the Forest, and the area is peppered with oil and gas wells. Nevertheless, the area is so large, extending over 800 square miles, that there is ample opportunity for hikers, backpackers and ski-tourers to sense remoteness and solitude. Deep within the Forest itself may still be signs of man's past activities, such as old logging roads, camps, and railroad grades, but they are gradually being reclaimed by the forest. In fact, the off-trail hiker can make good use of the old roads and grades.

The U.S. Forest Service does not own all the land within the administrative boundary of the Forest. The parcels of non-public land (inholdings) include whole municipalities such as Sheffield and many small lots with hunting cabins and vacation lodges. Of interest to hikers are Chapman State Park and the two Pennsylvania State Game Lands within the Forest. These are Game Lands No. 28, which occupies 14.2 square miles in the southern region of the Forest and Game Lands No. 29, covering 14.5 square miles south of Warren. Other State Game Lands extend the effective hiking area beyond the Forest boundary. For example, on the west side of the Allegheny River upstream from Tidioute is Game Lands No. 86, while adjoining the southern boundary of the Forest are Game Lands 24 and 44. Hiking is possible on State Game Lands, but camping is prohibited. On the northern boundary of the Forest, in New York State, Alle-

Hiking across a meadow in the lower reaches of the Allegheny Front area.

gany State Park covers 105 square miles. These additional public lands, both within and beyond the National Forest boundary,
make the whole area very popular for vacationers and outdoor-
oriented people.

One of the unique features of Allegheny National Forest is
its so-called "savannah" areas. These flat, open areas occupy
about 4% of the Forest. When the timber on these areas was cut
early in this century, the water table rose to (or near to)
surface level because trees were no longer available to transpire moisture back into the atmosphere. As a result of the
high water table, trees have great difficulty regenerating in
these areas. Visitors will find savannah areas along Bear
Creek Trail, in Hickory Creek Wilderness and elsewhere. Scattered trees, occasional giant stumps from early in this century, grassy meadows, meandering streams, marshland wildlife
and park-like grassy side slopes make savannahs interesting
places to visit. Spring and fall are the best times to visit
them because the shortage of shade often makes summer visits
uncomfortably hot. As trees grow up around the edges of the
savannahs the water table drops, producing more trees. So the
savannahs are shrinking, decade by decade. The Forest Service
has identified key savannah areas where this unique quality is
to be maintained through special management practices.

Another "interesting" feature of Allegheny National Forest
is the tornado damage that occurred on May 31, 1985. About $10
million worth of timber was destroyed and a great blue heron
rookery was wiped out. About 21 square miles of forest was destroyed or damaged, including one square mile of Hickory Creek
Wilderness and a third of the Tionesta Scenic Area. Some of
the swaths are about a mile wide, and the destructiveness of
the tornado-force winds is still obvious and awesome. Trees in
the middle of these swaths were literally ripped to shreds--
even their trunks. Trees at the edge of the swaths were bowled
over like match-sticks. The USFS has built road-side overlooks
at some of the better vantage points. The sharpness of the
edges of the tornado swaths is also amazing. Trees a few yards
away from the swath edges appeared virtually untouched, while
trees a few yards into the swaths exist now only as stumps top-
ped by ragged splinters where the tornado plucked off the top
like someone might pluck a flower. Trails across tornado
swaths were usually rendered impassable. These trail segments
were rerouted where possible, or abandoned. The Trail Notes
section of this Guide describes the current status of all
trails. So don't assume the trail you walked before June of
1985 will still have the same route. Some of the maps in the
Trail Notes sections show the boundaries of tornado swaths.

Other special features of the Allegheny National Forest
include the Tionesta Scenic Area, the Tionesta Research Natural
Area, and the Heart's Content Scenic Area. These areas feature

some of the oldest and largest tracts of virgin beech-hemlock forest in the eastern U.S. They offer the public a rare opportunity to view unique ecosystems. The ANF also features the Kane Experimental Forest. This 2.6 square-mile tract is administered by the Northeast Forest Experimental Station as an area of research on forest management practices.

The New Allegheny National Forest Land Management Plan

A land management plan is required for each national forest by the Forest and Rangelands Renewable Resources Planning Act of 1974 (RPA), as amended by the National Forest Management Act of 1976 (NFMA). The purpose of the plan is to provide direction for multiple use and sustained yield of goods and services from national forest lands in an environmentally sound manner. The land management plan for Allegheny National Forest and its Environmental Impact Statement (EIS) came out in April of 1986 after a planning process that began in the early 1980s and which involved much public input. Some features of the Plan which are of interest to the recreational forest visitor are described below. The planning process is mandated to be repeated every 10-15 years, but each plan looks 5 or more decades into the future. The ANF Draft Plan, with its EIS, cover 800 pages.

Wilderness and National Recreation Areas

The Plan assumes that the Wilderness issue has been settled for the next decade by the Pennsylvania Wilderness Act of 1984, which established 15 square miles of Wilderness (Hickory Creek and some Allegheny River islands) and 36 square miles of National Recreation Areas (NRAs) on the ANF (the Allegheny Front Area between Allegheny River and PA 337 west of Heart's Content, and an area on the east side of Allegheny (Kinzua) Reservoir). So it considers no other possibilities for these two land classifications which now occupy 6.5% of the ANF. The Plan calls for vegetation in the NRAs to progress through a process of natural succession to mature and over-mature hardwoods. Timber harvesting will be only for wildlife habitat improvement or to satisfy recreational objectives. NRA roads will be closed to the public and used only for wildlife habitat improvement activities. Emphasis there will be on dispersed recreation, and off-road vehicles (ORVs) will be excluded.

Oil and Gas Mitigation Areas

A minor, but innovative, part of the Plan calls for mitigating the effects of intensive oil and gas development on 3.1 square miles of the ANF by allowing the forest to progress via natural succession to mature and over-mature hardwood and softwood forests. No timber harvests will occur except for salvage of diseased or damaged trees. Unnecessary local roads will be closed and revegetated. Emphasis will be on dispersed recreation, with only minimal investment in, and management of, recreational facilities.

Special Areas

Four especially unique areas (Tionesta Scenic Area, Tionesta Research Natural Area, Hearts Content Scenic Area and Kane Experimental Forest) will continue to be managed in a way that protects their uniqueness and scenery, while allowing scientific research to be carried out. These areas total 9.4 square miles. Another 1.6 square miles will continue to be devoted to high-density recreation developments (campgrounds, beaches, boat launches, picnic areas, etc.). Another 1.6 square miles (Buzzard Swamp) will be devoted almost exclusively to wildlife habitat. It has a high population of a wide variety of wildlife.

Big Timber Area

A 7.8 square mile area of the ANF will be devoted to an innovative experiment in forest management. Timber will be harvested on 80-160-year rotations rather than the normal 70-100-year rotations. And there will be no timber harvesting during 30 years of each 40-year period. So the area could well develop into one noted for a healthy diversity of scenic, wildlife and recreational values, plus high quality timber. Roads will be closed during 30 of every 40 years. Recreational use of the area will be mainly hiking backpacking, ski-touring, hunting, fishing and primitive, dispersed camping. ORVs will not be permitted. The area is immediately southwest of Twin Lakes Campground and Beach. It contains the Mill Creek Loop (hiking) trail and the northern end of Bear Creek informal trail. It is at the headwaters of scenic Mill Creek--important as a water supply for communities further south. The area will also be valuable for evaluating the economics of growing high quality sawtimber on long rotations on national forest lands.

--And More Big Timber

The areas described above total 75 square miles--less than 10% of the ANF. But another classification--some 169 square miles (21% of the ANF)--will be devoted to "a land condition with vegetation generally progressing through natural succession to mature and over-mature hardwood forest." Timber harvesting will be limited--mainly to that thought desirable for wildlife habitat improvement and recreation quality. Management will emphasize wildlife species that benefit from mature or over-mature hardwood forest (e.g. bear, turkey, squirrel, cavity-nesting birds). Emphasis will also be on dispersed recreation activities in a semi-primitive motorized setting.

Sawtimber Production Areas

Most (520 square miles--2/3 of the ANF) will be managed as sawtimber and wildlife production areas. Selection cutting will be done on 9.4 square miles and over 25 square miles will be in old-growth timber (150 years and older). The rest will be subject to clear-cutting and shelterwood removal when trees reach 70-100 years of age. Clearcut size is limited to a maximum of 40 acres. Historically, clearcuts in the ANF have averaged between 20 and 25 acres, and the Forest Service plans to

maintain this average size. The Plan states that emphasis will
be on "high quality" sawtimber. Critics have pointed out that
rotation ages of 70-100 years are too short to grow "high quality" (large diameter) sawtimber for most hardwood species.
Cutting on longer rotations could produce a greater dollar-
value of timber sales receipts per acre per year on a sustained-yield basis while enhancing the diversity of scenic values, wildlife habitat and recreational values.

The plan calls for increasing timber harvesting rates by
45% in the first decade and by 100% by the fifth decade as the
sustained-yield capacity of the ANF is approached. The USFS
justifies these increases by pointing out that a disproportion-
ately large fraction of trees on the ANF are in, or approach-
ing, the 70-90-year age range.

Trails

The Plan calls for construction of 48 miles of foot trails
and 156 miles of motorized trails over the next decade.

Roads

The Plan calls for a major increase in road construction.
Public comments on the Draft Plan objected strongly to this
construction. In the Plan the Forest Service noted that about
70% of the road construction will involve low-standard roads
which will be used in timber sales and then closed and seeded
after each sale is completed.

Vegetative Diversity

The composition of timber types under the Plan will remain
about the same as it is today. If management direction were
continued over the entire 150-year planning horizon, the forest
would be composed of the following timber types:

Allegheny hardwoods (Cherry, Maple, Ash, Popular)	51%
Oak	18%
Northern hardwoods (Sugar Maple, Beech, Birch)	16%
Savannahs	4%
Conifers	4%
Wildlife Openings	5%
Aspen	2%

Resort Development on Allegheny (Kinzua) Reservoir

The Plan calls for a motel/restaurant complex adjacent to
Kinzua Beach on Allegheny Reservoir. This would be developed
by private capital by 1996. The majority of the public re-
sponse to this issue in the Draft Plan opposed this development
and favored retention of the reservoir's natural character.
There is reason for concern. Allegheny Reservoir, for the most
part, is surrounded by steep hillsides, so public access is
very limited. Private waterfront resort-type developments are
prone to flashing neon signs, loud music, etc., and these could
significantly degrade the quality of reservoir aesthetics.
Also, the public could, over time, find its access limited to
only a very few (and less desirable) spots along the reservoir-
-the reservoir their tax dollars paid for--if developers get a
camel's nose under the tent and then apply political pressure

A small falls on crystal-clear Big Mill Creek as it runs through a hemlock grove near Ellithorpe Run and the junction of Bear Creek Trail and Mill Creek (loop) Trail.

to the U.S. Forest Service for more "privacy" for their paying guests. The USFS argues that it can control the character of resort-type developments with restrictive leasing arrangements. But whether the USFS can resist, for all time, the intense political pressures that well-funded developers are able to exert remains at least open to question.

An economic study found that a "small rustic resort" of the type envisioned by the U.S. Forest Service would not be economically viable. If so, after construction, the USFS would be subject to intense pressure to allow all manner of other developments on the site of the "small rustic resort" to amuse guests and bestow "profitability." Wouldn't it be better to place a full-scale commercial resort a mile from the reservoir and have a small tramway to whisk paying guests to and from a private sun deck that gives access to the public beaches, boat launches, and scenic views that the reservoir now offers everyone?

Foot Trails in National Forests--A Perspective

Foot trails are an important part of most national forests. Table I, below, may be of interest to those familiar with other national forests in the eastern U.S.

Table I - A comparison of the sizes of the National Forest trail systems in various eastern states (1978 data unless otherwise indicated)

State	N.F. Area (sq.miles)	Trail Miles	Miles of Trail per Sq. Mile	Notes
Maine	33.0	80	2.42	
New Hampshire	437.8	1055	2.41	
Vermont	167.4	353	2.11	
Virginia	1025.8	2101	2.05	(1987 data)
North Carolina	733.5	1454	1.98	(1987 data)
Tennessee	396.9	553	1.39	
West Virginia	851.2	817	0.96	(1987 data)
Indiana	115.5	57	0.49	
Michigan	1729.0	680	0.39	
Ohio	106.6	42	0.39	
Kentucky	381.2	140	0.37	
Minnesota	1782.5	581	0.33	
Missouri	818.6	245	0.30	
Pennsylvania	798.4	226	0.28	(1989 data)
Wisconsin	955.3	181	0.19	
Totals	9622.1	7672	0.80	

The national forest trail situation, as a whole, is disturbing. Over the past five decades, trails on the national forests have decreased from 0.55 mile per square mile to 0.34. Over this same period, national forest roads have increased

from 0.24 mile per square mile to 1.01. The plot below shows
these trends. (Data came from a 6/1/85 study by Wells Associates Inc., 5180 NE Sullivan Road, Bainbridge Island, WA 98110.)

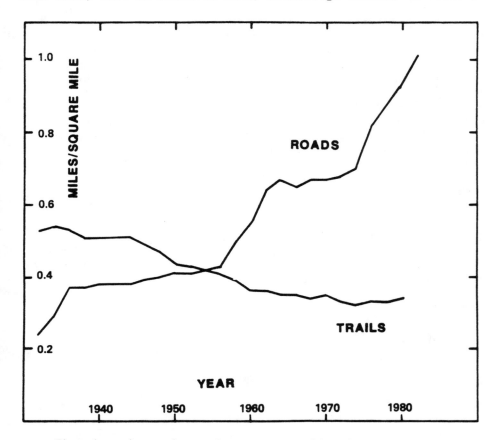

The plot above shows the most startling increases in national forest roads during the past decade. This trend threat-
ens to continue, since many recent (1985-87) national forest
land management plans have proposed massive increases in road
construction. During this same decade, the plot shows trail
mileages leveled off, reflecting the slashing of USFS trail
budgets. Forest Service budgets now lump road- and trail costs
into one number, making it hard for citizens to interpret USFS
plans.

Massive road-building programs threaten the scenic- and
natural charm of national forests. They endanger wildlife
species such as turkey, bear, and others. They pose the threat
of massive increases in taxpayer-subsidized (below-cost) timber
harvests. More importantly, they threaten our future. All
eleven major studies of western national forests acknowledge,
tacitly or explicitly, that present timber harvest rates cannot
be sustained much beyond the end of this century. Eastern na-

tional forest managers measure tree growth in ways more appropriate to pulp wood in order to justify wasteful harvests of immature sawtimber. The U.S. Forest Service is one of the more open, responsive federal agencies. Use your hiking experiences on the Allegheny National Forest to develop a well-reasoned vision of what the future of the Forest should hold--and voice it whenever the USFS solicits public opinion.

Trees of the Allegheny National Forest

The Changing Composition of Allegheny National Forest

Tree Species	"Original" Abundance*	Present-Day Abundance**
Beech	31%	4%
Hemlock	27	3
Sugar Maple	13	7
Birch	6	5
White Pine	6	0
Chestnut	6	0
Ash	1	3
Black Cherry	0.1	33
Aspen	?	4
Red Maple	?	27
Oaks	0.6	5
Totals	91%	91%

* H. J. Lutz, Journal of Forestry, 28 (1930) p.1098-1103
** USFS data. Also see Forest Statistics for Pennsylvania-
   1978 USDA-FS Research Bulletin NE-65

Common Trees Native to Allegheny National Forest

Amer. bittersweet	Hawthorne	Oak, black
Apple	Hazelnut, American	" , chestnut
Ash, white	Hemlock	" , red
Aspen	Hickory, shagbark	" , scarlet
Azalia	Holly, large leaf	" , white
Basswood	" , winterberry	Pine, pitch
Beech	Hop-hornbeam	" , white
Birch, yellow	Ironwood	Rhododendron
Black gum	Juneberry (shadbush)	Sassafras
Butternut	Maple, mountain	Sour gum
Cherry, black	" , red	Speckled alder
Cherry, choke	" , silver	Spice bush
Chestnut	" , striped	Sycamore
Cucumber magnolia	" , sugar	Tulip-tree
Elm, American	Mountain ash	Willow, pussy
" , slippery	Mountain holly	Witch-hazel
Dogwood, flowering	Mountain laurel	

13

Ferns of the Allegheny National Forest

Adiantum pedatum	Maidenhair fern
Dryopteris austriaca	Spinulose shield-fern
Dryopteris marginalis	Marginal shield-fern
Dennstaedtia punctilobula	Hay-scented fern
Cinnamomea	Cinnamon fern
Osmunda clayloniana	Interrupted fern
Onocelea sensibilis	Sensitive fern
Polystichum aerostichoides	Christmas fern
Pteridium agulinum	Bracken
Thelypteris noveboracensis	New York fern

Wild Flowers of the Allegheny National Forest

Actaea rubra	Red baneberry
Aralia nudicaulis	Wild sarsaparilla
Arisaema atrorubens	Jack-in-the-pulpit
Aster umbellatus	Aster
Coptis groenlandica	Goldthread
Odulophyllium thalictroides	Blue cohosh
Claytonia virginica	Spring beauty
Dicentra cucullaria	Dutchman's breeches
Disporum	Fairy bells
Erythoronium americanum	Dogtooth violet
Fragaria	Strawberry
Galium	Bedstraw
Gaultheria procumbens	Teaberry
Hepatica	Hepatica
Habenaria orbiculata	Round-leaved orchid
Kalanthemum vanadense	False or wild Lily-of-the-valley
Mitella	Miterwort
Mitchella repens	Partridgeberry
Medeola virginiana	Indian cucumber-root
Oxalls	Wood sorrel
Phytolacea americana	Pokeweed
Polygonatum	Solomon's Seal
Potentilla	Cinquefoil, five-finger
Rumex acetosella	Sheep sorrel
Ranunculus	Buttercup
Trientalis borealis	Star-flower
Trifolium	Clover
Trillium	Wakerobin, birthroot

Saxifraga	Saxifrage
Smilax herbacea	Carrion-flower
Smilacina	False Solomon's Seal
Solidago	Goldenrod
Stellaria	Chickweed
Viola	Violet

Wildlife of the Allegheny National Forest

The Forest provides a range of habitat for a diversity of wildlife. At least 46 different mammals, 217 bird species, and 71 species of fish are found in the area. Several wildlife species within the range of the Forest require special attention. The Indiana Bat is classified in the Federal Register as endangered and although not yet observed, the expected range covers this area. The River Otter and Bobcat also require special attention based on present population sizes. Six species of fish that are found in the Allegheny River drainage area have been classified as rare or endangered in Pennsylvania. They are the Allegheny Brook Lamprey, Tippecanoe Darter, Long-head Darter, Slenderhead Darter, Brook Stickleback, and the Southern Redbelly Dace.

Among the game species, the white-tailed deer is the most important and abundant, while small game and wild turkey attract the largest number of hunters. The black bear population provides 12 percent of the total bear kill in the state. The most common fur-bearing animals are beaver, mink, muskrat, opossum, raccoon, red fox, skunk, and weasel.

Deer of the Allegheny National Forest

For the visitor to the ANF, deer are a mixed blessing. Deer are everywhere--and there are far too many of them relative to the capacity of the land to support them. They add interest to a hike. They add to the risks of driving vehicles in the ANF since they are inclined to jump out in front of your moving car. When you drive (or hike) through the ANF watch for the "browse line"--the total absence of vegetation (other than tree trunks) up to about 5 feet above ground level. This means that deer are destroying the habitat for many other species of wildlife ("cottontails," snowshoe hares, grouse and many others--even black bear). It also means that new trees under 5 feet tall don't have a chance of becoming big trees. It means that some species of vegetation are being driven to extinction in the forest. It also means mass starvation of deer in the early spring of each year. It also means hunters harvest only scrawny runts. (There have been years when the largest deer shot in Pennsylvania weighed under 100 pounds. Average adult bucks should weigh about 140 lbs. (dressed))

15

Plastic shields protect young tree sprouts on a clear cut in
Allegheny N.F. The Forest's excessive deer population is making
tree regeneration impossible, wiping out a number of plant
species and destroying the habitat of several other kinds of
wildlife.

Watch also for assorted desperate measures of the Forest Service to regenerate new forest on cut-over land. You will see high deer fences and even plastic enclosures around individual trees. These methods, like spraying deer repellent, really aren't economically feasible, even though the ANF produces some of the most valuable timber species grown anywhere in the U.S. Foresters estimate that there may be 32-40 Virginia white-tailed deer per square mile in parts of the ANF. The land, on average, can support about 20 deer per square mile without any of the problems mentioned above. (Young hardwood forests can support about 40 deer per square mile on browse; mature forest can support about 20 deer per square mile on "mast" (acorns, beechnuts, etc.), while middle-aged (pole) forest can only support about 10 deer per square mile since it offers neither browse nor mast.)

The history of Pennsylvania's deer population is plotted in Figure 1. Recall that deer were nearly wiped out by the deforestation around the turn of the century. But after that the population exploded, and by 1928 we were learning an important lesson in wildlife management: you can't control populations by hunting only males. An earlier "Bucks Only" law was repealed and the first doe hunting season was held in 1928 (over furious opposition, some of which persists even to this day). Note that we have never had a stable deer population in this century. ANF studies (involving enclosing various numbers of radio-collared deer in deer-proof pens on clearcuts) show that the State Game Commission significantly under-estimates deer populations.

In parts of the ANF the composition of the forest is being modified by deer. Trees like yellow poplar, cucumber tree, white ash, black cherry, northern red oak, eastern hemlock, red maple, and sugar maple are being replaced by ferns, grasses, sedges, beech and striped maple--species that deer find less tasty. These changes decrease the natural diversity of our forest lands, besides being very costly to the timber industry.

Birds of the Allegheny National Forest

Approximately 130 species of birds, ranging in size from the Ruby-throated Hummingbird to the Turkey Vulture, have nested in the Forest. The Tionesta Natural and Scenic Areas are of special interest since they favor those species which live and breed in a virgin forest habitat. Also to be noted are State Game Lands #28 and #29, where Turkey Vultures and Wood Ducks are at home, and the Buzzard Swamp Area, southeast of Marienville and the Owls Nest Area east of S.G.L. #28, where birds such as Canada Geese, Kestrels, Mallard, and Marsh Hawks may be spotted. On Allegheny Reservoir, the Common Loons and Bald Eagles are occasionally reported. Ospreys have been sighted on both the Clarion and Allegheny Rivers. Chapman Dam State Park is a good place to see Ospreys and Whistling Swans.

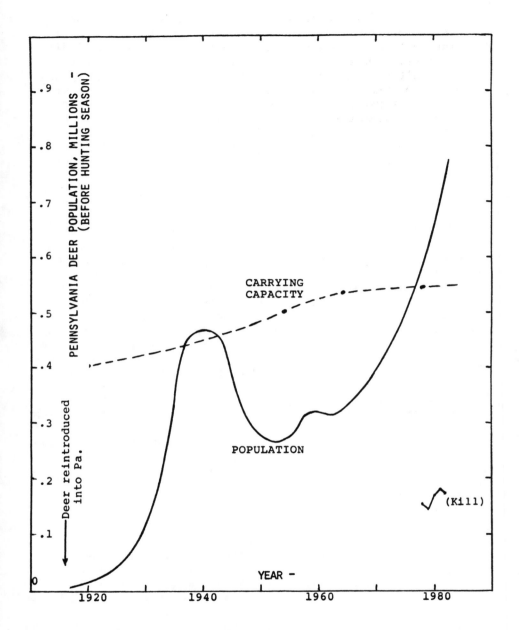

History of Pennsylvania's deer population (adapted from work by
Leopold and by Bennet, plus Game Commission data. Current
problems with excess deer are mainly in the northern half of Pa.
Also shown is an estimate of the number of deer the land resources of Pa. can support without major adverse environmental
effects. In the late '60s the Game Commission stated that
350,000 was the best herd size for Pa. Kill data include road-,
hunter-, farmer- and illegal kills but not starvation.

18

Near Buckaloons camping area Green Herons, Red-tailed Hawks and migrating Warblers may be sighted.

Amphibians and Reptiles of the Allegheny National Forest

When walking through the Forest don't forget that the ground under your feet, the leaves you shuffle through, and the decaying logs are not only part of the cycle of energy for the Forest, but are also habitat for a variety of creatures. Under logs and log fragments are found the all-black, white-spotted amphibian, the Slimy Salamander (Plethodon glutinosus) and the Red-Backed Salamander (Plethodon cinereus cinereus). Another reptile found in wooded areas is the Coal Skink (Eumeces anthracinus), a small brown lizard which has a thick black line bounded by two thin white lines, running from behind the eye down onto the tail. Snakes found in the Forest include the Black Rat Snake (Elaphe obsoleta obsoleta), the Eastern Garter Snake (Thamnophis sirtalis sirtalis) and the Milk or House Snake (Lampropeltis doliata triangulatum). The latter can be distinguished by a pattern of blotches bordered by black on a whitish or greyish background. It is often mistaken for the poisonous Copperhead (Agkistrodon contortrix mokeson), a snake with a coppery head and hourglass-shaped bands across the back, from side to side, with the band narrowest in the center of the back. The only other poisonous snake (besides the copperhead) in the Forest is the Timber Rattlesnake (Crotalus horridus horridus), recognized by black crossbands edged with white on the back and sides, and the rattle. Both poisonous snakes tend to hibernate, sometimes sharing the same den, along rocky ledges. Water snakes include Ribbon-Snakes (genus Thamnophis), slender snakes with narrow stripes of different colors running the length of the body. Look for them where crayfish populations are high. The Northern Water Snake (Natrix sipedon sipedon) is found in larger streams and rivers. It has a dark pattern on a light background. The patterns on the sides and back meet. It is the only large water snake in this part of the country.

Along the edges of small streams both frogs and salamanders can be found. Some that prefer these habitats are the Dusky Salamander (Desmognathus fuscus fuscus) and the Mountain Dusky Salamander (Desmognathus ochrophaeus). Both have highly variable markings. Older adults are dark brown with a pattern of fainter markings on the back. Among frogs and toads expect the American Toad (Bufo americanus) which is dark-brown to olive-green or grey with darker spots of black or brown. Females often display patches of lighter (buffy) colors. The Wood Frog (Rana sylvatica) can be identified by a dark "mask" around the eyes. It ranges from green to light-brown in color.

Several other frog species can be found in watery habitats. The following prefer ponds: Leopard Frog (Rana pipiens)--spotted. Pickerel Frog (Rana palustris)--squarish dark spots. Green Frog (<u>Rana clamitans melanota</u>)--variable pattern but usually bright green and brown, and the Bullfrog (<u>Rana catesbiana</u>) which is distinctive because of its large size and nearly plain green color.

Respect for these amphibians and reptiles is essential. They should not be removed, collected, killed or harmed in any way, for they play an important and fascinating role in the ecosystem.

Some Thoughts on Snake Bites

Current field therapy for snake bits is to immobilize the bitten area, usually an arm or leg. Pack the area in ice if available, perhaps in the car on the way to the hospital. A clean compress soaked in icy water from a clean mountain stream will help. A constrictor band may be applied, but only lightly. The blood flow to the area must not be stopped. The band may be released slowly every 15 minutes for a minute or so. Since venom remains in the area of the bite for 6 to 8 hours, a constrictor band may not even be necessary. Do not make cuts, as some kits may instruct. Attempts can be made to suck the venom from the bitten area. The puncture wounds must be kept clean, for infection may become a more serious problem than the venom. Obtain professional treatment as quickly as possible, but never make the victim move rapidly. This will only make the heart pump faster, circulating more blood to the area. The side-effects of antivenin (snake bite medication) may be more serious than the poison, so many hospitals admit and observe the victim, avoiding use of the drug if possible. No amateur should make haphazard use of antivenin. Prior tetanus immunization, important for every outdoorsperson, or a tetanus booster at the hospital are more valuable. Statistics are overwhelmingly in favor of the safety of the visitor to the Allegheny National Forest. Most of the 14 or so snake bite deaths in the United States each year occur in the South, where the snakes are more numerous and more potent. Only 3% of rattlesnake bites are fatal in the U.S. It would take the combined venom of ten of our local copperheads to kill one 150-pound man. Of course, the venom will be proportionately more dangerous to a small child. To avoid snake problems, develop the habit of looking where you place your hands and feet, especially near rocks or logs. Remember that poisonous snakes are shy and generally strike only when cornered.

Geology of the Allegheny National Forest

The Allegheny High Plateau was formed by the uniform upward movement of sedimentary rocks, free of folds and faults. On the top of the plateaus, the bedrock types are of the Pennsylvania Period (280 to 310 million years ago). The deeply eroded valleys that dissect the plateau cut into formations from the older Mississippian Period. Further below, but exposed by glacier action in the northern part of the Forest, are rocks of the Devonian Period (350 to 400 million years ago). The rock formations contain an abundance of sandstone and shale and are roughly divided as follows.

a) The Pottsville formation is a yellowish-gray strongly acid, coarse textured, thick horizontally bedded sandstone. But also included are thin strata of gray quartz conglomerate, some greenish gray, coarse textured shales, and a few thin coal beds.

b) The Pocono formations are thick horizontally bedded, yellowish to greenish gray, strongly acid, coarse textured sandstone with interbeds of gray quartz conglomerate. The lower strata of the formations are less acid, finer textured and more green in color.

c) The Oswayo formations are thick greenish-gray sandy shales with interbedded shales and frequently fossiliferous sandstone layers.

d) The Cattaraugus formations consist of medium acid, coarse textured shales and thin strata of fine textured sandstones and some pink quartz conglomerate. The top members of these formations are greenish to brownish green, changing to brown or reddish brown in the middle and lower sections.

Below is a map of the physiographic provinces of Pennsylvania.

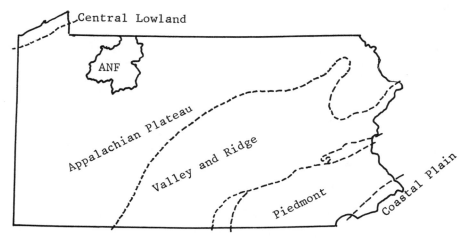

Central Lowland

ANF

Appalachian Plateau

Valley and Ridge

Piedmont

Coastal Plain

Location of the Allegheny National Forest relative to the Physiographic Provinces of Pennsylvania.

Oil and Gas Issues in the Allegheny National Forest

The Allegheny National Forest lies in the heart of Pennsylvania's oil and gas region, only 40 miles from the site of the first U.S. oil well. In 1981, 17% of the State's crude oil production came from mineral rights owned by private individuals within the Forest boundary. Because of its high paraffin content, Pennsylvania crude is one of the world's best lubricating oils. In 1981 15,000 wells were in operation on the ANF. Over 100,000 wells have been abandoned (and left unplugged) during the past century.

Currently only 6% of the mineral rights under the ANF are in public ownership, and mineral rights give their owners the right to damage land surface features while prospecting and extracting minerals. Visitors to the ANF often become quite familiar with the oil and gas industry. Half-buried, rusting pipes travel along many of the corridors (old logging roads, hiking trails) used by hikers. Drilling access roads, pumps, pipeline corridors, storage tanks and settling ponds (for brine pumped up with the oil and gas) are common in many parts of the ANF--as are stream pollution and the odor of oil and gas. In some areas the industry provides the forest visitor with interesting peripheral attractions. In other parts of the ANF the industry's visual impact is obnoxious.

Waterways of the ANF are in the uppermost reaches of the Allegheny River watershed which provides drinking water for a significant portion of western Pennsylvania. So water quality degradation by the oil and gas industry in the ANF is of broad public concern, and millions of dollars are spent annually in efforts to clean up after the industry. The brine and other pollutants pumped into streams and aquifers from oil and gas wells can be fatal to wildlife and domestic animals.

About half of the oil and gas originally under the ANF has been removed--the easy half. Many of the remaining drilling operations are currently economically marginal and retain economic viability only through public subsidies in terms of environmental degradation (e.g. surface water pollution, ground water pollution, erosion from poorly built access roads). The real balance sheets are all in red ink for many of these operations. In decades past, Pennsylvania's laws governing oil and natural gas development were among the weakest in the nation. Around 1985, new state laws were passed to protect the public from industry excesses.

Long-term trends in the oil and gas industry in the ANF threaten virtually all the environmental values the public currently associates with the ANF. The last remaining oil and gas in the ANF will require "secondary" and "tertiary" recovery technology. (Secondary recovery methods have been used in the ANF to a limited extent for some years now.) These methods involve forcing water or steam (and eventually a variety of exotic chemicals) into about 80% of the wells in order to draw oil and gas out of the remaining 20% of the wells. Tertiary recovery involves massive arrays of pumps, chemicals, tanks, settling ponds, tangles of pipes--and grids of roads spaced perhaps 100 yards apart. Threats to water quality (ground water and surface water) could be devastating, and reasons for visiting the ANF could nearly vanish. The ANF offers one more reason for supporting public policies that encourage energy conservation. If the extraction of the remaining oil and gas under the ANF could be spread out over many generations the ANF would always offer what it offers today. In addition, total receipts from sales of its oil and gas reserves would be greater, as would the total value of these extracted minerals to the consuming public.

Streams and Rivers of the Allegheny National Forest

The Forest is on the Allegheny plateau. In general, the lay of the land is determined by how deeply this plateau has been cut by the streams and rivers. Thus some of us are inclined to say that there are no hills in this part of Pennsylvania--only valleys. As illustrated in Map 1, the center of the Forest contains the numerous headwaters of Tionesta Creek and the terrain is relatively gentle. To the east are the headwaters of an Allegheny River tributary, the Tunungwant, flowing north, and tributaries of the Clarion River flowing south. Elevation changes are moderate. The western and northern borders are dominated by the Allegheny River valley, where the most dramatic scenery is found. The heights above the valley provide fine views. The neighboring country, roughened by numerous sidestreams and rivers feeding the Allegheny, also offers visual rewards.

Climate of the Allegheny National Forest

Because the Forest lies in the path of many storms that cross the country from west to east, sudden weather changes occur throughout the year. The average annual precipitation for the Forest is comparable to that for the state as a whole. Long term records show 41 inches at Ridgway in the southeast, 43 at Warren and Tionesta on the Allegheny, and 45 inches near Kane and Allegheny Reservoir towards the northeast. Over the years, the annual totals have ranged from 30 inches to 60 inches. The average yearly snowfalls range from 60 inches in the southern portion of the Forest to 100 inches in the Allegheny Reservoir area. Snowfall and days with snow cover vary over the Forest much more than does the total annual precipitation.

The combined effects of latitude, generally high elevation, and radiation conditions, make the Forest area one of the coldest locations in the State. Severe weather is uncommon to the area, although thunderstorms can be accompanied by strong winds and hail. Tornados also occur in the Forest.

A savannah along Bear Creek Trail. (The wheel measures trail length.) Photo by Derrell Weilacher.

HIKING, BACKPACKING AND SKI-TOURING IN ALLEGHENY NATIONAL FOREST

Contacting the U.S. Forest Service

At various points in this Guide you are referred to the U.S. Forest Service in the Allegheny National Forest. The addresses and telephone numbers you will need to do this are given below. Normal office hours are 8:00 AM to 4:30 PM.

Forest Supervisor
Allegheny National Forest
222 Liberty St. P.O.Box 847
Warren, PA 16365
814-723-5150

Ridgway District Ranger
Allegheny National Forest
Montmorenci Road (PA948)
Ridgway, PA 15853
814-776-6172

Bradford District Ranger
Allegheny National Forest
Star Route (PA59 & PA321)
Bradford, PA 16701
814-362-4613

Sheffield District Ranger
Allegheny National Forest
Kane Road, Route 6
Sheffield, PA 16347
814-968-3232

Marienville District Ranger
Allegheny National Forest
State Highway 66
Marienville, PA 16239
814-927-6628

The Kinzua Point Information Center (KPIC) is also a valuable source of information. They are located 15 miles east of Warren on PA 59. They are open seven days per week from Memorial Day through Labor Day and are open on weekends in May, and September through October 15. Their telephone No. is 814-723-1291.

Opportunities for Hiking

Perhaps the only type of hiking that is not possible in the Allegheny Forest is the kind of mountain walking, above the tree-line, to be enjoyed, for example, in New Hampshire and the western states. Otherwise, there is a continuous spectrum of hiking possibilities from an evening stroll along a quiet, unpaved Forest Service road to the 20-miles-a-day trail-bashing exercise. This guide describes the opportunities for hikes that take more than one hour. Some of these hikes require preparation, perhaps even conditioning, but they enable one to explore the forest and enjoy its scenery in an unhurried and uncrowded fashion.

The hiking trails maintained by the U. S. Forest Service
are:
A. North Country Trail. . . . . 88.0 miles
Northern ANF: (33.9 miles total)
A. Tracy Ridge Trail. . . . .   6.5   "
B. Tracy Ridge Ski-Touring Trail   3.5   "
C. Land of Many Uses Interpretive Trail . .   2.0   "
D. Rimrock Ski Trail   2.5   "
E. Rimrock-Morrison Trail (loop). . . . . . 12.3   "
F. Campbell Run Interpretive Trail   1.5   "
G. Longhouse Interpretive Trail . . . . . .   1.1   "
H. Westline Ski Trail   4.5   "
Southeastern ANF: (42.3 miles total)
A. Black Cherry Trail . . . .   1.6   "
B. Twin Lakes Trail   12.7   "
C. Mill Creek Trail (loop). . . . . 16.7   "
D. Tionesta Scenic Area Interpretive   1.0   "
E. Laurel Mill Ski-Touring/hiking Trails. . 10.3   "
Southwestern ANF: (65.5 miles total)
A. Minister Creek Trail (loop) . . . . . .   6.6   "
B. Tanbark Trail   8.8   "
C. Tidioute Riverside Rec-Trek Trail. . . .   2.5   "
D. Hickory Creek Trail (loop)   11.1   "
E. Hearts Content Scenic Area Trail . . . .   1.3   "
F. Hearts Content Ski-Touring Trail   7.7   "
G. Buckaloons Seneca Interpretive Trail . .   1.0   "
H. Deerlick Ski-Touring Trail   7.6   "
I. Beaver Meadows Loop Trail System . . . .   6.1   "
J. Loleta Hiking Trail   3.5   "
K. Songbird Sojourn Interpretive Trail. . .   1.7   "
L. Buzzard Swamp Ski-Touring Loop Trails   7.6   "

_____

       Total USFS-Maintained Foot Trails   =   229.7 miles

     The locations of these trails are indicated in Map 2 along
with the principal roads in the Forest. The principal trail,
the North Country Trail, has been developed as a section of the
proposed National North Country Trail that may eventually join
the Appalachian Trail.

Informal Trails
       There are trails in the ANF that are not maintained by the
USFS, but which are in good condition and of exceptional scenic
value. Several of these trails are in the southeastern portion
of the ANF. This area is devoid of USFS-maintained trails despite two prime attractions--Bear Creek and Clarion River. For
people from southwestern Pa. and central Pa., this area also
involves less driving time than the remainder of the Forest.
       The Bear Creek Trail runs along Bear Creek from Mill Creek
(loop) Trail to the Clarion River. The Clarion River Trail

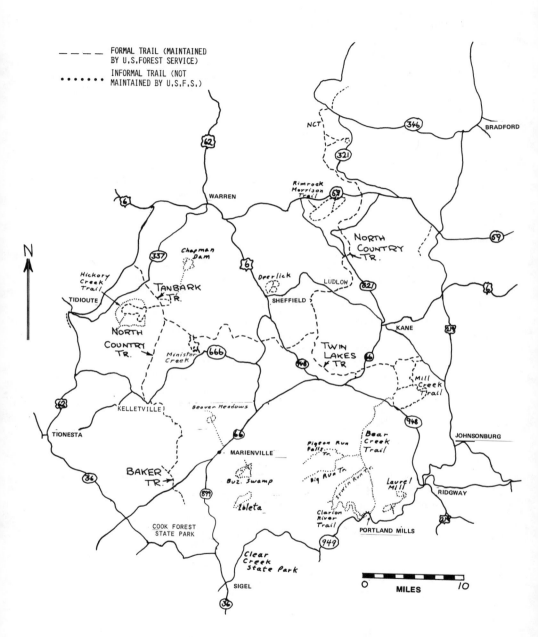

FORMAL TRAIL (MAINTAINED BY U.S.FOREST SERVICE)

INFORMAL TRAIL (NOT MAINTAINED BY U.S.F.S.)

BRADFORD

NCT

WARREN

Rimrock Morrison Trail

NORTH COUNTRY TR.

N

Chapman Dam

Hickory Creek Trail

TIDIOUTE

Deerlick

LUDLOW

SHEFFIELD

TANBARK TR.

KANE

NORTH COUNTRY TR.

Minister Creek

TWIN LAKES TR.

Mill Creek Trail

KELLETVILLE

Beaver Meadows

TIONESTA

Bear Creek Trail

MARIENVILLE

Pigeon Run Falls Tr.

JOHNSONBURG

BAKER TR.

Buz. Swamp

Big Run Tr.

Irwin Run Tr.

Laurel Mill

RIDGWAY

Ibleta

Clarion River Trail

PORTLAND MILLS

COOK FOREST STATE PARK

Clear Creek State Park

SIGEL

0   MILES   10

MAP 2 – MAIN ROADS AND HIKING TRAILS OF ALLEGHENY NATIONAL FOREST

runs along the banks of the Clarion River from Bear Creek to Irwin Run. Irwin Run Trail goes up Irwin Run from the west end of the Clarion River Trail to near Bear Creek Picnic Area (roughly the midpoint of Bear Creek Trail). The three of these trails form a loop that offers an excellent location for a three-day backpacking trip, or even for a week-long backpack trip when used in conjunction with Mill Creek Trail and Twin Lakes Trail. Big Run Trail and Pigeon Run Falls Trail travel up scenic stream valleys to Owls Nest and down to Bear Creek Picnic Area.

Off-Trail Hiking

A main attraction of the Allegheny National Forest is the opportunity for enjoyable off-trail hiking. The numerous old logging roads and railroad grades, most commonly found in the stream valleys, are useful for planning cross-country hikes. However, such hikes should only be attempted by those who are competent in the use of map and compass, and plenty of time should always be allowed for stream crossings, unexpected detours, and back-tracking. (In 1989 the Forest Service started to remove cable bridges across streams whenever gas companies lack interest in maintaining them, partly due to the potential for legal liability if someone falls off one.)

Among the areas that are particularly suitable for this type of hiking are the relatively large roadless areas of the Allegheny Front, Buzzard Swamp, Clarion River, Hickory Creek, Salmon Creek, and Tracy Ridge. The approximate locations of these areas are indicated in Map 3. They are described in the Trail Notes. Also of interest are the ANF's Management-Category-6.2 areas. These semi-primitive, non-motorized areas are also shown on Map 3.

Some Hints for Hikers and Backpackers

Personal preference has a lot to do with hiking habits, so little can be said here that is not disputable. Enjoying hiking and backpacking often involves revising basic attitudes. The most common attitudes needing to be corrected are:
(1) that hiking involve some sort of struggle between man and nature, and man must be prepared to "beat nature into submission" in order to enjoy hiking:
(2) that a major purpose of hiking is to cover as many miles per day as possible, and
(3) the more (company) the merrier.
Much space could be devoted to presenting the case against these myths. Rather than that, the following suggestions are offered for consideration.
(1) Never carry an ax, hatchet or similar tool. (You do not need them; they are dangerous and heavy.)

28

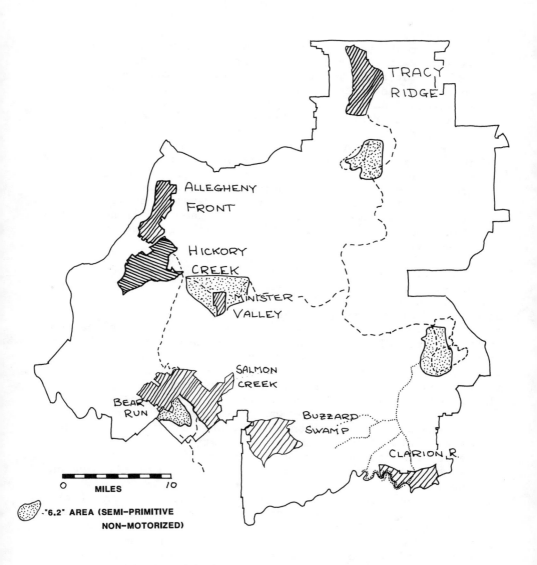

TRACY
RIDGE

ALLEGHENY
FRONT

HICKORY
CREEK

MINISTER
VALLEY

SALMON
CREEK

BEAR
RUN

BUZZARD
SWAMP

CLARION R.

0   MILES   10

-"6.2" AREA (SEMI-PRIMITIVE
       NON-MOTORIZED)

MAP 3 – HIKING TRAILS AND ROADLESS AREAS SUITABLE FOR BACK-COUNTRY HIKING

29

(2) Carry a minimum of gear, and take simple, readily prepared
    foods. But be prepared for accidents and bad weather.
(3) Keep camp fires small. Never prepare a new site when an
    old one is available. Use only backpacker stoves for cook-
    ing. Go to bed early and get up shortly after sunrise.
    (You will hear and see more wildlife, get better photo-
    graphs, and do a larger fraction of your walking before it
    gets hot.)
(4) Take a break whenever the whim occurs to you. Go for a
    wade or swim in a mountain stream. Explore interesting
    rock formations. Try to get artistic photographs. Lie on
    your back and listen to the birds and the wind. Take a
    leisurely lunch break. Try to identify plants, trees,
    birds, foot-prints, etc. Ten miles per day for a hike and
    8 for a backpack trip should be regarded as reasonable.
    You should be able to keep yourself occupied with interest-
    ing pursuits even when you cover only half that distance.
(5) Keep your group size down to 6-8 or less. Solve your
    group's shortage-of-leadership problem in some other way.
    A car shuttle and the economics of travel to and from the
    area will recommend two car-loads of people. If no shuttle
    is needed, one car-load is better. Hiking alone, though
    pleasant, can be risky.

    The Allegheny National Forest is within a day's drive of a
sizeable fraction of the population of the U.S. Lots of people
visit it, and use is bound to grow heavier over the coming
decades. Your enjoyment of the ANF is made possible by the
care that visitors before you exercised, and by the dedication
of USFS personnel. Ethically, then, you have the same obliga-
tion to the visitors who follow you as those before felt toward
your visit. In case you're wondering how to exercise your
social conscience, below are a few suggestions.
(1) If you packed it in, pack it out. And, for good measure,
    pack out some litter that was not yours. If carrying it
    all the way home is inconvenient, drop if off at a dumpster
    at a developed campground or any District Ranger Station.
(2) Leave gates the way you found them; stay away from farm
    animals; don't damage fences or walls, even by climbing on
    them.
(3) Don't contribute to erosion by cutting across switch-backs
    or by using boots with excessively deep lugs on the soles.
(4) Camp at least 60 yards from any trail, lake, stream or
    meadow and out of sight of the trail. Avoid camping on
    especially scenic areas such as meadows, cliff edges and
    beds of wild flowers. Leave your campsite looking more
    natural than when you arrived.
(5) Enjoy flowers, plants, animals and minerals in their natu-
    ral setting--not by taking them home with you.
(6) Never cut boughs for a bed. Never dig hip-holes for sleep-
    ing, or trenches around your tent.

(7) On every trip, clear some fallen limbs from the trail (leaving those that are lying flat on the ground).

(8) Solitude is fragile. Bring no radios; keep your group size small. Avoid crowds by planning spring-, fall- or mid-week trips and by seeking out less-well-known areas.

(9) Never put soap, food particles, or body wastes in or near water bodies.

(10) Use backpacker stoves instead of cooking fires. Substitute warm clothes and small campfires for ordinary clothes and large campfires. Use established fire sites whenever possible. Repackage unused food rather than discard it.

(11) Dig latrines for feces and toilet paper at least 6 inches deep--and at least 50 yards from trails, campsites, or water bodies.

(12) Report trail conditions to the district ranger in writing. (See addresses on page 25.) Report the nature and location of major problems in detail.

What to take Hiking and Backpacking

Below is a checklist of items to consider.

One-Day Hikes:

Knapsack
Matches (waterproof)
Waterproof poncho or rain suit
Rain Chaps
Hiking shoes or boots
Trousers: Denim dungarees in
  summer, Army mountain pants or
  loose-fitting dungarees
  and longjohns in winter
  (never tight levis)
First aid kit: chapstick, water
  purif. tablets, bandages, burn
  ointment, gauze, salt pills,
  moleskin, adhesive tape, anti-
  septic, aspirin, insect
  repellent, sunscreen/block

Hat or cap with brim
  (avoid sunburn)
Lunch
Flashlight (small)
Canteen of water
Pocket knife
Windbreaker, full zipper
  parka (not coated),
  or two or more light
  jackets or sweaters
  in cold weather
Maps (in plastic bag)
Compass
Sunglasses (a must for snow)
Candle
Plastic garbage bag (count-
  less uses)

The new fabric-and-leather boots are generally quite comfortable and easy to break in, but they are not much cheaper than all-leather boots and do not provide as much support or last as long. If you want total waterproofing, choose boots with Gore-Tex lining, but do not expect them to breathe away much foot perspiration, despite advertized claims. This is because you should treat any leather boot with a good preservative agent (Sno-Seal for example) to prevent the leather from drying out and cracking.

It is important that you have totally waterproof rain gear. You can spend hundreds of dollars for fancy Gore-Tex gear, but a $30 poncho-and-chaps outfit will serve you nearly as well in all but the most extreme conditions.

Backpacking Trips:
　　(Same as for one-day hikes, except replace the knapsack by a backpack and frame and consider the following):

Sleeping bag

Plastic sheet (ground-cloth)

Sleeping pad

Tent or a large piece of heavy plastic or coated nylon with reinforced holes than can be pitched as a rain shelter (less than 3 lbs. per person of capacity)

Cord (50' of 1/8"-3/16" nylon for a variety of uses)

Extra jacket(s) or sweater(s)

Pot(s) (light-weight)

Stove (backpacker) with fuel in leak-tight container

Scouring pads

Cup (large, unbreakable, doubles as a dinner plate)

Toilet paper (1/3 roll/week)

Bandana

Spare flashlight bulb,battery

Socks, 2 pair (cotton inner, wool outer) minimum

Change of socks (plus 2 pair for sleep wear)

Mittens (not gloves) in cold weather

Towel (small), wash cloth

Soap

Pencil stub

Notebook (small)

Spoon

Food (compact, dry, not easily spoiled) (2 lb./ person/day maximum)

Garbage bag(s) (plastic)

Luxury items: swimsuit, camera, binoculars, paperback book, nature-study guide, shoulder pads for straps of pack frame.

　　A bewildering array of backpacks is available today. Which one you choose depends on the kind of use it will receive. If you plan on doing a lot of off-trail rambling or ski-touring, your best choice would be an internal-frame design. These provide a lower center of gravity and more freedom of movement in tight situations. Internal frames, however, simply do not transfer their weight to the hip belt as effectively as the more traditional external frame models.

　　Two basic types of sleeping bags are suitable for backpacking; those filled with goose- or duck down, and those filled with various types of polyester fiberfill (Polarguard, Hollofil, Quallofil, etc.). Both can be bought in a range of sizes from tight mummies to full rectangular depending on how much elbow room you feel you need. Down bags are undoubtedly warmer for their weight, more compressible and more durable than synthetic bags. They are somewhat more expensive to buy. But in the long run they are cheaper to use. However, down has a distinct disadvantage for Appalachian backpacking: it sops up water and perspiration like a sponge, and dries only very slowly. By contrast, polyester absorbs little moisture and dries quicker. This is a critical point because eastern mountains, from spring through fall, are often quite humid, and once a down bag becomes damp it is almost impossible to dry in the field. And no matter how carefully you protect the down

A small stream and pond among the tall trees of Heart's Content Scenic Area loop trail.

from external wetness, you cannot avoid dampening it from perspiration. This may not greatly affect the warmth factor of
the down, but it does mean that, on long trips, you are going
to end up feeling as though you've been sleeping in a warm
swamp.

A modern backpacking stove is not only a great convenience
but it is also less intrusive on the local environment, by
eliminating the need to burn wood for cooking. Any decent
white gas or butane stove will suffice. Gas stoves are hot and
efficient, but are fussier than butane stoves. Remember,
butane fuel will not burn if it is below freezing.

A sleeping pad should be considered standard equipment.
Few tent sites are soft enough to make it possible to sleep
well without one. They also provide significant under-body
insulation.

Many excellent books deal with equipment for hiking and
backpacking. Among them: <u>Backpacking: One Step at a Time</u>
(1980) by Harvey Manning, and <u>The Complete Walker III</u> (1984) by
Colin Fletcher.

Especially during hunting season, especially, and at all
times in remote areas, wear bright-colored outer garments for
safety: reds, oranges, and yellows (for safety).

It is standard practice to pack out all unburnable rubbish
in plastic garbage bags. "Pack it out" is a rule stressed in
all national parks. The importance of this has increased
greatly in recent years due to the popularity of backpacking
and because of the decrease in the number of areas suitable for
backpacking. "Leave nothing but foot prints; take nothing but
pictures, kill nothing but time" is the first rule of backpacking.

Food for Backpackers

The cost of dried and freeze-dried food from outdoor
stores is quite high. In the interests of convenience and
economy, obtain backpacking food from supermarkets as much as
possible. For weekend trips there is no need to go to an outdoor store. To obtain sufficient variety on a week-long trip,
a few freeze-dried items may be necessary. Below is a partial
list of backpacker foods available from supermarkets.

GORP*** ingredients: Cheese (durable, low-fat variety)*
   Nuts*   "Familia", "Grainola", etc.
   Dried fruit   Powdered Milk **
   Chocolate   Peanut Butter *
Margarine (calories) *   Dried peas, beans, etc.
Instant puddings   Sausage (spiced)
Instant cheesecake   Canned nut-roll
Dried (thin) beef   Soups (dried)
Potato flakes   Powdered lemonade, etc.
Rice (instant or reg.)   Cocoa

Macaroni & cheese dinners	"Instant Breakfast"
Spagetti	Dried eggs
Instant oatmeal	Cookies
Pancake mix	"Pop-Tarts"
Crackers	Fruit cake
Coffee	Gravy (powdered)
Cream (powdered)	

* In cold weather, greater fat intake is essential to maintain comfortable body temperature.
** Order powdered <u>whole</u> milk ("Milkman" Brand) from western U.S. suppliers.
*** "<u>G</u>ood <u>O</u>ld <u>R</u>aisins and <u>P</u>eanuts"
    Green beans and snow peas keep quite well and are good raw or cooked. Normally, appetites are below normal the first few days of a backpacking trip. After that, appetites grow to above normal. Plan menus accordingly.

When to go Hiking

    Many would dispute the premise that there is a "best" time to go hiking in the Forest, for each season has its own attractions. Spring is a time of year when the woods have an obvious beauty. To some hikers the Forest is at its best just before the leaves come out in May, when the ground is covered with blooming "pre-vernal flora" and unobstructed views are possible through the stands of unleaved trees. Summer has the advantage of needing less equipment--lighter and cheaper. What is an easy stroll in the summer can take on the proportions of a major expedition in the depths of winter. For some, the Forest is too crowded in summer. For others it is too hot, although the nights are rarely uncomfortable. The popular fall colors reach their gaudy peak in early October and the woods are perhaps most colorful for the few remaining days that the ferns and brackens are still green.
    While the spring has its vitality and summer has its lushness, the late autumn is gentler and more subdued. When shrouded with mist on an early November morning the Forest appeals to a different mood. Later in the year the hiker should be wary of hunting season. If the urge to walk in the woods during hunting season is irresistible, then try to go out only on Sundays. If this is not possible, at least wear a brightly colored safety jacket and hat. (Orange is preferred.) Hiking in winter has a different set of rewards. The Forest is transformed into another world when the skies clear to a brilliant blue after a heavy snowfall. With a ground cover of snow there is a hushed quality to the woods, as long as the snowmobiles and ATVs are far enough away. And with a snow cover the visitor is easily able to appreciate the amount of wildlife activity there is in the Forest, an appreciation that is harder to come by in the summer months. Although problems with icy

roads are encountered, winter offers more by way of broad
views.

Campsites

A list of 17 maintained campgrounds is included on the
official administrative map of the Forest, obtainable for $2.00
from Allegheny National Forest, P.O. Box 847, Warren, PA 16365.
Campgrounds vary in size and facilities from the "suburban"
variety containing more than 90 sites to much smaller camps
along the Allegheny Reservoir that can only be reached by boat
or foot. In addition to the Forest Service campgrounds, a
maintained campground is found at Chapman State Park (814-723-
5030), located west of Clarendon, which is south of Warren on
US 6. In the areas surrounding the Forest there are numerous
private campgrounds, as well as public campgrounds at Clear
Creek, Elk and Cook Forest State Parks and at Tionesta Dam and
East Branch Dams.

Camping is allowed within the Forest itself. However,
sites should be at least 500 yards from roads. Around Allegheny and Tionesta Reservoirs, camping is not allowed in the
forest within 500 yards of the shoreline.

In accord with backpacking ethics and the Forest Service's
"No Trace" guidelines, the following is suggested.
1) To prevent site overuse and water pollution, avoid camping
   within 100 feet of streams.
2) Use open fires and campfires only as an emergency source of
   heat. Cook using backpacker stoves. If a fire is abso-
   lutely necessary, use an old fireplace rather than prepare
   a new fireplace.
3) For the disposal of human wastes, "emulate the cat" well
   away from streams.
4) Carry all rubbish out in plastic garbage bags.
5) Limit the group size to six persons or less. This will
   minimize your impact on the camp area.

On page 37 is a list of formal campgrounds in the ANF, along
with some information on size and fees as of summer 1990.

Water Quality

In the Trail Notes later in this Guide are comments on
water available for drinking. These comments are based only on
surmises made by trail scouts, based only on their impressions
of what lies upstream. (Dwellings and pastures will generally
disqualify a potential source of drinking water.) In no case
are these comments based on any sort of chemical analysis or
bacteria count. You should know that serious diseases can be
carried in unpurified streams and springs and rely only on your
own judgement in each case. No guarantees of any kind are

REC AREAS	Camp Sites	Camping Fee (1)	Toilets: Flush/Vault (1)	Handicapped toilets	Showers	Drinking Water (2)	Dump Station	Group Sites (2)	Play area, Picnic Sites: # people (3)	Swimming	Day Use Fee (4)	Fishing	Boat Launch	Trails (5)	Interpretive Programs	Opening Dates (6)	Closing Dates (6)
Beaver Meadows	36	Lo	V			H			2			●	–			4	12
Buckaloons	51	Lo	FV	●	●	PH	●	50	15			●	–			4	10
Dewdrop	74	M	F	●		P						●	–			5	9
Elijah	10	NC	V													4	12
Handsome Lake*	26	NC	V			H						●	●	H		4	12
Hearts Content		Lo	V			H			11					H		4	12
Hooks Brook*	20	NC	V			H								H		4	12
Hopewell*	8	NC	V			H										4	12
Jakes Rocks			FV	●		H			34			●		H		4	12
Kiasutha	92	Hi	F	●	●	P	●		110	●	$2	●	–			5	9
Kinzua Beach			F		●	P			130	●	$2	●	●		●	5	10
Loleta	32	Lo	FV	●	●	PH	●	100	40	●	2-3	●	●			4	12
Minister Creek	6	Lo	V			H						●		H		4	12
Morrison*	32	NC	V			H								H		4	12
Old State Road*	28	NC	V			H										4	12
Pine Grove*	28	NC	V			H										4	12
Red Bridge	55	M	FV	●	●	PH	●					●	●			4	12
Rimrock		NC	V			H			30			●				4	12
Roper Hollow		NC	V													–	–
Tidioute		NC	V													–	–
Tracy Ridge	120	Lo	V			H	●	100	5			●		H		4	12
Twin Lakes	45	Lo	FV	●	●	PH	●	100	50	●	2-3	●	HI		●	4	12
Webbs Ferry	70	M	FV									●	H			–	–
Willow Bay			FV	●	●	PH	●		114			●	H			4	12

* boat access only

(1) Lo = Low rates ($5-7);
M = Medium rates ($7-10);
Hi = High rates ($10-12);
NC = No Charge.
NOTE: Checkout time is 2:00 p.m.

(2) Pressure System or Handpumps

(3) $25.00 per day

(4) $2-3/car; or $1/person on foot, bicycle, etc.

(5) H = Hiking or backpacking trail;
I = Interpretive trail;

(6) Opening and closing date codes correspond to month numbers as follows:

OPENING DATES:
4 = April 15
5 = Thursday before Memorial Day weekend (May)

CLOSING DATES:
9 = Tuesday after Labor Day weekend (September)
10 = Monday after the last weekend in Sept (Sept/Oct)
12 = End of Antlerless Deer season (mid-December)

MORE ABOUT SEASONS:
Regular Summer Season is from Memorial Day weekend to Labor Day weekend (codes 5-9). Facilities open before or after these dates have limited service and lower rates during the off-season. No snowplowing will be done.

During the off-season, flush toilet systems are shut down and there are no showers. Drinking water is usually shut off before first frost. Kinzua Beach has no bathhouse or other facilities after Labor Day

37

implied in this Guide. Using one's own judgment is risky at
best, so always carry a canteen.
     Below are four ways of treating water for drinking pur-
poses. All produce a certain amount of "off-taste".
(1) Boil for one minute. To restore taste, pour rapidly back
     and forth between two containers to re-aerate it.
(2) Place 8 drops of a 2.5% iodine solution in a quart of
     water and let stand ten minutes. A druggist can prepare
     the solution for you.
(3) Place one "Halazone" (R) tablet in a pint of water. Dis-
     solve completely. Let stand 30 minutes after the tablet
     has dissolved. Buy tablets from a drug store. They dis-
     solve only slowly in cold water.
(4) Add 16 drops of fresh household "Clorox" to a gallon of
     water and let stand for 30 minutes. Then smell the water.
     If there is no chlorine odor, re-treat the water.
     Human enteric diseases have been acquired in remote wild
areas from water contaminated by wildlife. You won't necessar-
ily get hepatitis, but you could get a 24-hour vomiting-diar-
rhea syndrome that could leave you dangerously dehydrated and
too weak to carry a backpack.
     Methods 2,3, and 4 may not necessarily inactivate viruses
capable of causing enteric disease, particularly hepatitis,
giardiasis, and polio. Boiling is the safest method.
     Several water purification systems are now on the market,
priced from $35 to $300, which perform well and are not heavy.

Maps
     Topographic maps can be obtained from the U.S. Geological
Survey. Printing and Distribution Center, Denver Federal Center Box 25286 Denver, CO 80225 (303-236-7477). The cost is
$2.50 per map(1988); discounts are available for large orders.
First order an index to Topographic maps of Pennsylvania and
the Survey's free leaflets: "Topographic Maps" and "Topographic
Maps-Silent Guides for Outdoor Men". Topographic maps are
indispensable on any hike. Even if one knows the trail well,
topo maps can suggest interesting side trips and alternative
routes. Besides, one might find oneself in sudden need of a
short cut. The Trail Notes in this Guide are written under the
assumption that the appropriate topo map(s) is visible to the
reader. The 15' series topographic maps of the ANF are out of
date. Use 7.5' maps. The grid of 7.5' maps that covers the
area covered by this Guide is provided in Map 4. The appropriate topo maps for particular sections of trail are indicated in
the Trail Notes.
     The full usefulness of this Guide is realized only after
the reader has obtained, from the U.S.Forest Service (P.O. Box
847, Warren, PA 16365), the following map:

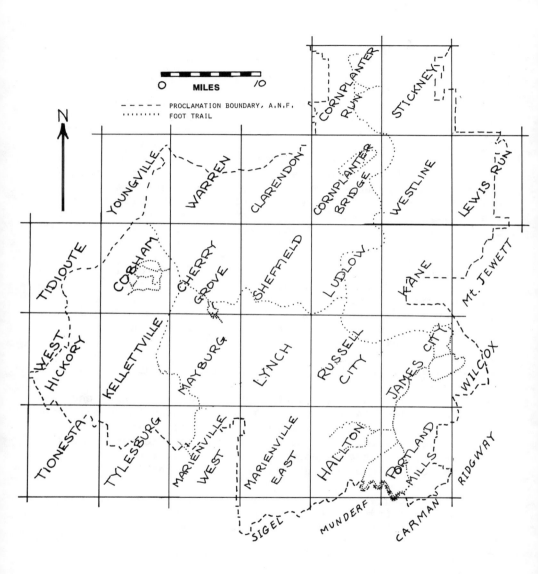

MILES

- - - - - PROCLAMATION BOUNDARY, A.N.F.
·········· FOOT TRAIL

N

CORNPLANTER RUN

STICKNEY

YOUNGVILLE

WARREN

CLARENDON

CORNPLANTER BRIDGE

WESTLINE

LEWIS RUN

TIDIOUTE

CORHAM

CHERRY GROVE

SHEFFIELD

LUDLOW

KANE

Mt. JEWETT

WEST HICKORY

KELLETTVILLE

MAYBURG

LYNCH

RUSSELL CITY

JAMES CITY

WILCOX

TIONESTA

TYLESBURG

MARIENVILLE WEST

MARIENVILLE EAST

HALLTON

PORTLAND MILLS

RIDGWAY

SIGEL

MUNDERF

CARMAN

MAP 4 – GRID OF 7.5' U.S.G.S. TOPOGRAPHIC MAPS COVERING ALLEGHENY NATIONAL FOREST

<u>Forest Administrative Map</u> (1974--limited revision in 1987)
A map of the entire Allegheny National Forest at a scale of
1/2"= 1 mile. It shows most of the roads and trails, public
ownership, lakes, streams, recreation sites. (No contour
lines) $2.00 each.

<u>Off-Road Vehicles</u>
        Certainly some of the most agonizing problems facing pub-
lic land managers, law-enforcement agencies, property owners,
and those seeking to enjoy the peace and serenity of the
forests and countrysides have arisen with the increased use of
trail bikes, snowmobiles, and ATVs in recent years. "No Tres-
passing" signs are going up; sections of major hiking trails
that cross private land are being closed down by irate landown-
ers, and ever-tighter restrictions are being placed on the use
of such vehicles. By now there are few who have not heard the
protests and arguments concerning these vehicles--the damage to
plant and animal life, the erosion of trails and hill sides,
the vandalism at remote structures and fences, the disturbances
to the tranquility of rural and wooded areas, and any number of
others.
        Before purchasing an ORV, consider the following:
(1) A noise level of 80 decibels is sufficient to cause
     (eventually) permanent damage to the human ear.
(2) Telephone guy wires are almost capable of almost decapi-
     tating people traveling at snowmobile speeds. Barbed-wire
     fences, deep ruts, etc. can inflict serious injuries.
(3) Cars, trucks, buses, and locomotives have run down ORV
     users unable to hear their approach.
(4) Mechanical breakdowns in remote areas can cause serious
     problems.
(5) At least one Michigan doctor of considerable experience in
     the problem claims that all snowmobile users have hairline
     cracks in their backbones after three or fewer seasons.
(6) The trailer for one's car, the numerous other accessories,
     the repairs, the maintenance, and the storage often make
     the cost of owning and operating ORVs much higher than one
     anticipates.
(7) Much of the appeal of most remote areas arises from the
     peace and tranquility found in these areas.
(8) Struggling to get ORVs over fallen logs, across deep
     ravines, etc. is hard work.
(9) Some boggy areas in the Allegheny National Forest have been
     reduced to ugly quagmires by heavy ORV use.
(10) The injury rate for drivers of three-wheeled ORVs is ex-
     tremely high.

        There appears to be some progress in reducing conflicts
between ORV users and the public. ORV organizations have
developed, and are promoting, a "Tread Lightly" program to

More boulders and ferns along Tanbark Trail.

41

teach "Light on the Land" techniques for reducing environmental damage and improving their public image.

Much more comprehensive discussions of issues related to the use of ORVs on public lands are available. A good one is "Off-Road Vehicles on Public Land" published in 1979 by the Council on Environmental Quality. Obtain copies from the U.S. Government Printing Office, Washington, DC 20402 (Stock No. 041-011-00041-6). This report contains a bibliography of 193 publications of studies of the effects of ORVs.

The USFS annually reviews its "Road and Trail Management Program," which governs the use of all types of motorized vehicles on Allegheny National Forest roads and trails. Information on the current policy is available from the Forest Supervisor (address on page 25). The public is invited to participate in the review and revision of this program. Also available from any ANF office are free maps of ORV trails in the ANF.

The Allegheny National Forest Needs You!

In 1972, Congress passed special legislation to enable interested citizens to assist in the important conservation work of the Forest Service. If you are people-oriented and are concerned about natural resources and environmental quality, the Allegheny National Forest needs your skills and talents in its volunteer program.

Anyone may apply. The volunteer program has something for about everyone--retirees, professionals, housewives, students, teenagers, and youngsters. Volunteers under 18 must have written consent from a parent or guardian. Retired professionals have a wealth of knowledge they may wish to share.

You can choose to be involved in outdoor work with other volunteers working in building and maintaining trails, rehabilitating campgrounds, improving wildlife habitat, and performing other conservation projects. Also, you may have a special interest, such as archaeology or geology, where your skills can be utilized and your knowledge enhanced by working with professionals on the staff.

Much satisfaction can be gained from helping others to understand America's heritage and natural resources. If you are interested, contact the Forest Supervisor's Office, P.O. Box 847, Warren, PA 16365 (814-723-5150) or one of the District Ranger offices in the area where you wish to serve and ask for an application. (addresses on page 25) Be sure to indicate any special interest area in which you wish to be involved or special skills you wish to use.

Your hiking group may also be interested in the Forest Service's "Adopt-A-Trail" program in which a responsible group volunteers to maintain sections of trails on the ANF according to guidelines provided by the U.S.Forest Service. For more information contact the Forest Supervisor's office in Warren (address above) or one of the District Ranger offices listed on page 25.

A large fraction of the annual maintenance required by a trail can be done most efficiently by hikers themselves as they walk the trail. Carrying a long-handled pruner or a bow saw weighing only a few pounds and cutting branches, saplings and fallen logs is something almost any hiker can do easily, and without detracting noticeably from the pleasures of hiking. It's also easy to carry a plastic garbage bag for packing out rubbish from remote camping areas, trailhead parking areas, etc. Below are some hints for maintaining trails.

(1) Don't do any blazing. The USFS prefers to do this using standard paints, plastic markers and procedures that have been developed over the years.

(2) Don't remove logs that are lying flat on the ground on hiking trails. These help to reduce trail erosion and discourage trail bikers. (Remove all logs from ski-touring trails.)

(3) It's often faster and easier to pull a fallen log off a trail than to saw a section out of it.

(4) Cheap cotton gloves are often handy for trail maintenance- -especially when there is lots of maintenance to be done.

(5) Hatchets and axes are too heavy and dangerous for trail maintenance. An exception is the swedish bush ax which is under two lbs. and is recommended by professional trail maintenance people. Obtain these axes from forestry supply houses since they are rarely carried by hardware stores or gardening shops.

(6) Report major trail problems (large blow-downs, serious erosion problems, trail-sign damage, etc.) to the district ranger's office. In that way they can spend their limited resources on fixing trail problems instead of finding them.

The USFS cannot help but suffer from any solution to the federal budget deficit. Hikers, like everyone else, are simply going to have to learn to live with the new realities of public land management.

Help to Improve This Guide

The ANF trail system is not static. Every few years new trails are added, while other trails are abandoned. Also, many trail descriptions here are incomplete, and, despite our efforts, errors remain. The Forest Service has been cooperative in keeping us up to date on trail changes that it is aware of. But in the final analysis, the long-term quality and value of this guide depends largely on the feedback we receive from trail users. The original 1977 edition of this guide resulted from the scouting efforts of about 10 people. Since then the scope of this guide has expanded to the point where the "committee" approach to keeping this guide up-to-date is simply not feasible, nor is it efficient.

Thus an appeal is made here to all who use this guide to contribute their experiences and comments for inclusion in later editions. To encourage this, a free revised edition will be sent, as soon as it is printed, to anyone who has contributed new information, corrections, etc., that are used in the new edition. Send material to: Bruce Sundquist, 210 College Park Drive, Monroeville, PA 15146 or to the Sierra Club address on the title page of this Guide.

Topographic maps that you send will be returned within two weeks after being received. The same holds for literature you wish to make the editors aware of. Do not forget to include your name, address and the approximate date of the hike on which your material is based. The interests of accuracy and the editors' convenience are greatly served if you include a Xerox copy of whatever page(s) of this guide you think should to be updated, along with the appropriate notation as to where a correction, insertion, etc. should to be made (especially for maps). But this procedure is not necessary. (You could also say something like "Sentence 6, paragraph 3 of page 97 is incomplete and misleading. Replace it by.......").

Photographs are also needed. Ideally they should be glossy, black-and-white, about 5"x7". Unused photos will be returned. Photos used in a future guide will be paid for ($10 each, plus a free copy of the new guide). Acknowledgements will be given in the caption and the photo returned--but some time after the new edition comes out. Color slides can also be used. If your color slide is used on the front cover you will be paid $75 for the use of your slide.

Examples of new material:

- sources of water
- possible camp sites
- location of views
- interesting side trails
- especially scenic spots
- location of trail signs
- description of trailhead parking
- clarification of confusing text
- location of trail problems
- location of gates on roads

Ski-Touring in the Allegheny National Forest

Allegheny National Forest offers some of the best ski-touring in Pennsylvania because:

- It has large numbers of old logging roads and jeep trails;
- It lies in the Lake Erie snow belt (Northwest winds pick up moisture from the relatively warm waters of Lake Erie and dump it as snow in northwestern Pennsylvania.),
- The combined effects of latitude, generally higher elevation, and radiation conditions make the Forest area one of the coldest in Pennsylvania.

The northern part of the forest gets about 100 inches of snow annually, while the southern part of the forest gets around 60 inches (as compared to 40 inches in Pittsburgh and 130 inches

on the top of Laurel Ridge). Because of the cold temperatures,
snow tends to linger much longer than in most of the rest of
Pennsylvania, giving snow a chance to build up instead of melt-
ing between storms.

The ANF has a "Winter Activities Map" that shows snowmo-
bile- and ski-touring trails. (See page 25 for the address of
the USFS.) In addition, the ANF has free maps ofindividual
designated ski-touring trails. The ANF does not plow snow on
its roads. Only state roads and back roads used as school bus
routes are plowed.

Winter travel off regularly-maintained highways should not
be taken lightly, even if only a short ski trip is planned.
From early November to mid-April carry snow tires, blankets or
sleeping bags, a shovel, tire chains, extra food, and matches
in your car. If the weather begins to turn bad while you are
on the trail, and you are uncertain of your ability to continue
on foot or drive back to a highway, get out as soon as possible. Don't delay and get trapped.

The potential of the ANF for ski-touring is just beginning
to be recognized. Countless trails, unplowed USFS roads, inac-
tive logging roads, pipeline swaths, etc. offer delightful ski-
touring routes. Recently the ANF developed two trails specifi-
cally for ski-touring. So ski-touring trips to the ANF are
likely to be rewarding--and even more so if you are into
exploratory ski-touring. In this Guide is an attempt to assess
the potential of each hiking trail for ski-touring. Where possible, each trail is rated S1, S2, S3, and S4 (beginner intermediate, advanced, and not suitable) based on trail steepness,
width, rockiness, crookedness, stream crossings, etc. The elevation range for each trail is also given, permitting one to
make an approximate judgement of snow conditions.

The high elevation of the ANF also means that the terrain
is rugged, so trails can have steep spots. Stream crossings
that offer hikers only minor challenges can provide ski-tourers
with formidable challenges. In the Table of Trips, the number
of stream crossings is given as an aid to planning ski-touring
trips. Because of the steepness of the terrain and the frequent stream crossings, beginning skiers should stick to trails
rated S1 and to USFS roads.

Below is a list of ski-touring areas in the ANF that the
Forest Service sanctions or is aware of. Also included are
ski-touring areas in New York State's Allegany State Park,
adjacent to the ANF on the north.

Allegany State Park (New York)

• The Art Rosco Ski-Touring Area is exceptionally good, with
better-than-average snow cover due to its elevation. For snow
condition information, call 716-354-2182. A topo map can be
obtained from Allegany State Park, R.D.1, Salamanca, NY 14779
(716-354-2545) or from the Administration Building on Redhouse
Lake. Ski rentals and a warming hut are also available at the
Administration Building. Cabins are also available. Christian

Hollow Trail is considered to be the best. To get to the area,
get off the Southern Tier Expressway (NY17) at Exit 19 or 21
east of Jamestown.

Marienville Ranger District
• The Buzzard Swamp Cross-Country Ski Area offers 8 miles of
beginners' trails in a forest laced with ponds. To get there
take FS130 at the center of Marienville (the road between the
Gulf station and the Bucktail Hotel) for three miles and turn
onto FS376. This area is described and mapped (Map 22) in this
Guide.

Sheffield Ranger District
• The Heart's Content Scenic Area parking lot is the starting
point for several ski-touring trails. Loop trails include
Heart's Content (2.5 miles), Tom's Run (3.2 miles), Ironwood
(3.3 miles). The 11.5-mile Hickory Creek Hiking Trail is also
suitable for ski-touring for well-conditioned, experienced
skiers (because of its length and remoteness). To reach
Heart's Content Scenic Area parking lot, take Star Route 337
from Warren or Tidioute to the junction of Heart's Content
Road. Take this road 4 miles to Heart's Content. From Sheffield, take Austin Hill (Bull Hill) Road to Heart's Content
Road. (Total distance: 15 miles)
• Deerlick Trail (7.6 miles) is located near the Sheffield
Ranger Station at the end of Tollgate Road.
• Tidioute Riverside Rek Trek Trail (2.5 miles) is located
along the Allegheny River. The trailhead is at the PFC parking
lot by the Tidioute Bridge.

Bradford Ranger District
• Unplowed roads and trails in and adjacent to Tracy Ridge
Campground provide about five miles of beginner- and intermediate ski-touring trails.
• Rimrock Road, an unplowed three-mile road provides a six-
mile round trip with spectacular views. This trail is suitable
for beginner and intermediate skiers.
• Trails for beginners to experts start at Westline. They
range in length from one to 7.8 miles.

Ridgway Ranger District
• The Laurel Mill Cross-Country Ski Area offers 5.3 miles of
groomed trails and five miles of ungroomed trails for beginner
and intermediate skiers. To get there, take Laurel Mill Township Road, T-307, west out of Ridgway for three miles. These
trails are described amd mapped in this Guide. (See Map 23.)
Contact the Boot Jack Snow Gliders at 814-776-6285 for more
information and ski conditions.

WINTER DRIVING - Automobile First Aid and Related Precautionary Measures
        Car problmes can create all sorts of troubles on winter
outings--especially in remote areas. In winter, car troubles
are more probable and the consequences more severe. One way to

minimize havoc on multiple-car outings is to "caravan"--i.e.
have all cars keep within sight of one another. The first rule
of caravanning is that you are responsible for the car <u>behind</u>
you. One passenger (not the driver!) should keep track of the
car behind and the car ahead. Be especially careful at turns
to be sure that everyone is aware that the turn is being made.
Do not count on caravanning to the point of not telling every
driver the detailed route to the final destination.

Try to make certain that at least one car on each outing
is equipped with a modest amount of equipment for dealing with
car trouble. Below is a check list for your car emergency kit.
Most of it will fit into a box of modest size that you can
throw into the trunk of your car before the outing.

(1) Jumper cables (for a dead battery)
(2) "Emergency" tire chains
(3) Jack (and spare tire)
(4) Wheel wrench (bigger the better)
(5) Small can of penetrating oil (for recalcitrant wheel nuts)
(6) Kit for pulling and cleaning cable connectors on a battery
     (compact, cheap)
(7) Spare fuel filter (compact, cheap), plus the wrench and
     screwdriver needed for changing a fuel filter
(8) Gas (1 qt.) in a well-sealed, properly labeled container
     (Pour a small amount directly into the carburetor to start
     a car with a bad fuel pump, a bad choke, a leaky gas line,
     or a partially clogged fuel filter.)
(9) Flares and/or other signals for emergency stops
(10) Extra car key (pinned inside your shirt pocket)
(11) Spare fuses (compact, cheap)
(12) Emergency tow cable
(13) Spare fan belt (plus wrenches needed for changing it)
(14) Flashlight
(15) Electrical tape for patching a bad spark plug wire
(16) Sand (also weighs down a light trunk)
(18) Scraper for icy windows
(19) Dry gas (It takes about 1 hr. for dry gas to reach ice in
     a gas line.)
(20) Snow shovel
(21) Snow brush
(22) Can of oil for motor (1 qt.) with a pour spout
(23) Adjustable Pliers
(24) Screwdriver (standard and Phillips Head)
(25) Duct Tape (for a leaky radiator hose, etc.)
(26) Fuel Siphon
(27) Crescent Wrench
(28) Scrap wire or coat-hanger
(29) "Starting Fluid" (to spray into carburetor) (Beware! Fire
     Hazard.)

Someone on the trip should be capable of diagnosing simple
problems in trying to start a car--e.g. a bad connection on a

battery terminal, or a choke stuck in the wrong position, or a flooded engine.

An ounce of prevention..... So in the fall, check the fan belt, get a tune-up and (for 4-cylinder cars especially) get a valve adjustment. Also check the battery for its ability to hold a charge and the gas line for excessive rust on its outer surface. A small leak, even one too small to allow gas to leak in an obvious manner, can make it very hard to start the car. Keep the gas tank at least half-full in the winter to reduce the risk of a frozen fuel line. Remove and clean the fuel filter each fall if you don't get it replaced with each tune-up. At the same time, clean the dirt and gunk from the choke mechanism with a spray cleaner sold for that purpose. Fall is also a good time to lubricate your speedometer cable (See directions on the can of speedometer lubricant.) and your door locks (with a special graphite lubricant sold especially for that purpose), and to patch and paint rust spots before winter salt sprays get to them. In areas where salt is used on roads, cars usually rust out long before the drive system wears out. While you are at it, lubricate your door hinges and latch mechanisms and check the front tires for uneven wear, indicative of the need for a front-end alignment (which you may want to get while you're getting a tune-up and valve adjustment). If your drive wheels are under your trunk and only lightly loaded, put sand bags into your trunk for better traction.

Switching to a lighter weight oil (or one of the new synthetic oils) in winter could be a wise investment in terms of being able to start the car more easily.

Frozen locks are not rare in winter in this part of the country. Carrying a small can of lock de-icer in your pack is one solution. Alternatively, use a lighter or matches to heat your key.

Winter snows lay deep on the Allegheny N.F. Be prepared. Photo by Fred Feit.

TRAIL PATCHES FOR HIKERS, BACKPACKERS AND SKI-TOURERS

Peace Trails Patch

Anyone who has walked in the Allegheny National Forest or elsewhere in the upper Allegheny River watershed may now obtain an embroidered cloth sew-on patch to commemorate that hiking experience. The patch, shaped like a broad arrowhead, is about four inches long and three inches wide. On the patch is a green pine tree with four white roots displayed on a sky-blue field. At the base of the arrowhead, on an earth-tan strip, "Seneca Peace Trails" is displayed in white letters. Below that strip, "Allegheny Forest Lands" is displayed in green letters on a light-blue strip. The border of the patch is light tan embroidery. The sketch on page 51 shows the patch layout.

The symbolism of the patch is appropriate to the history of the indian tribes that once inhabited the upper Allegheny River watershed. Five nations united in the Iroquois Confederacy--Mohawks, Oneidas, Onongagas, Cayugas and the Senecas-- maintained peace over a wide region--along the Great Lakes as far as Illinois and as far south as Chesapeak Bay. The "Iroquois Peace" was established not only by force alone, but also by offering justice and reasonableness. To these indians, "peace" was the same thing as "the Great Law"--it was righteousness in action, the practice of justice between individuals and nations. The symbol of the Iroquois Peace was the white pine tree; its white roots, reaching to the four points of the compass, were paths that would lead the peace-loving people to the shelter of the branches, which signified protection and security afforded by union under "the law".

Patches may be obtained by sending $2.00 for each patch to: Allegheny Group, Sierra Club, c/o William Dzombak, 621 Spring Street, Latrobe, PA 15650. Checks should be made payable to Allegheny Group, Sierra Club.

North Country Trail Patch

Anyone who has hiked, skied or snowshoed the entire 95 miles of the North Country Trail in Allegheny National Forest may obtain an embroidered cloth sew-on patch to commemorate that hiking experience. The patch outlines the North Country Trail route in the ANF from the Baker Trail in the south to Allegany State Park in the north. The shape of the ANF proclamation boundary surrounds the trail route in this 3.5" circular patch (green lettering, blue border on a white twill background). These patches are available from the Allegheny Outdoor Club, c/o Don and Brita Dorn, Star Route, Box 476, Sheffield, PA 16347 (814-968-5759) or Charles and Marjorie Neel, Star Route, Sheffield, PA 16347 (814-968-5415). The price is $3.50 A copy of your trail log is also required.

A grassy lane through dense ferns and woods - North Country Trail NW of Minister Valley.

STRUCTURE AND USE OF THIS GUIDE

Maps and the Table of Trails

Map 2 on page 27 shows major roads and the locations of various "groups" of trails. Use Map 2 when using the Table of Trails or the Trail Notes.

On pages 60 and 61 is the "Table of Trails" that summarizes basic information on the trails described in this Guide. The idea behind this Table is that, along with a USFS map, it gives an overview of hiking opportunities. A trail can be chosen for further consideration without having to read all the Trail Notes. The Table of Trails divides the Allegheny National Forest into three sub-divisions: the northern section (north of US 6); a southwestern section (west of the road between Sheffield and Marienville via Lynch), and a southeastern section (the remainder of the Forest).

Column 1 of the Table of Trails gives the name of the trail. For formal (USFS-maintained) trails, the name is the same as that used by the USFS and seen on its sign posts. Column 1 also gives the trail symbol (3-5 capital letters in parentheses) which is used in Columns 2 and 6.

Column 2 of the Table of Trails gives the starting point and the finish point. These points are junctions with roads, junctions with other trails, or obvious landmarks--all of which can be recognized on the appropriate map. Trails are denoted through the use of the trail symbols defined in Column 1. The abbreviations US, PA, Rt., and FS refer to various kinds of roads, all easily recognized on the appropriate map. (See the list of abbreviations on Page 55 .)

Column 3 of the Table of Trails lists the ranger district(s) that the trail runs through. The following abbreviations are used:

  B= Bradford Ranger District   R= Ridgway Ranger District
  M= Marienville Ranger Dist.   S= Sheffield Ranger District

Column 4 of the Table of Trails gives the trail length in miles (and kilometers).

Column 5 of the Table of Trails gives additional comments for each trail. These are described by code letters defined below.

S1= Suitable for beginner ski-tourers
S2= Suitable for intermediate ski-tourers
S3= Suitable for advanced ski-tourers
S4= Not recommended as a ski-touring trail
B = Suitable for backpacking
I = Interpretive Trail
M = A topo map of the trail is included in this Guide

Column 6 of the Table of Trails lists intersecting trails and roads (information useful for planning hikes involving several trails). Intersecting trails are denoted by the use of the trail symbols defined in Column 1, while intersecting roads are denoted in the same way as in Column 2.

53

Column 7 of the Table of Trails gives the maximum and min-imum elevations (in feet) encountered on the trail. This helps hikers and ski-tourers gauge the ruggedness of the trail and the amount of annual snow fall.

Column 8 of the Table of Trails gives the number of stream crossings encountered along the trail. Stream crossings that use bridges are not counted, nor are streams that can normally be crossed with a single step. This information is primarily of value to ski-tourers and winter hikers, since rock-hopping entails added risks in winter.

Column 9 of the Table of Trails tells what page in this Guide contains the Trail Notes relevant to that trail, and what page to find the trail map on.

Column 10 of the Table of Trails tells you which maps in this Guide show the trail route.

Following the Table of Trails are the three main chapters of this Guide, labeled "Trail Notes". They summarize informa-tion like: how to get to and identify access points, what kind of trailhead parking is available, the location of springs, camp sites and points of interest, a description of the route and scenery, comments on the availability of water, necessary maps, and whatever else the trail scouts thought appropriate.

Using the Trail Notes and Trail Maps

The three chapters of Trail Notes, starting on page 63, comprise the bulk of this Guide. These Notes also contain topo maps of most of the trails covered by this Guide. These maps are printed at the end of each chapter. The arrangement of these topo maps is shown on Map 5 on page 58. The text of the Trail Notes is keyed to the topo maps using notations composed of letters enclosed in squares, e.g. $\boxed{D}$. Such notations ap-pear in both text and maps, so you can quickly relate a partic-ular discussion in the Trail Notes to the corresponding spot on the topo map. The topo map(s) on which a given trail appears is listed on the third or fourth line of the Notes on the trail in question.

In some cases a trail appears on more than one topo map. In such cases the first-appearing key symbol is followed by the number of the corresponding map, e.g. $\boxed{K}$ (Map 3). Subsequent map key symbols pertainent to the same map (Map 3 in this case) are not followed by the map number. The first occurrence of a key symbol found on a different map is accompanied by the new map number. This new map number, as before, applies to all subsequent key symbols until the map number changes again.

Trail routes are shown on the topo maps in this Guide by small, closed circles, e.g. ● ● ● ● ●. Side trails (typically abandoned logging roads, abandoned USFS foot trails, etc.) noted by trail scouts (and usually mentioned in the text of the Notes) are designated by small open circles, e.g. o o o o o o. Side trails that are unexplored are shown as only a few open

circles. Larger numbers of open circles indicate the approximate extent to which the side trail has been explored. These
side trail notations provide additional landmarks. People who
like exploratory- or off-trail hiking can use these side trails
as jumping-off points for their side trips. Beware: information on side trails is incomplete: do not expect to see o o o
on the topo maps for every side trail you see on your hike.

The Trail Notes contain standard abreviations to conserve
space and reduce verbiage. These abreviations are:

ANF	Allegheny National Forest
USFS	U. S. Forest Service (U.S. Dept. of Agriculture)
US19	Federal Highway 19 (or whatever the No.)
PA293	Pennsylvania State Highway 293 (or whatever the No.)
SR-20706	State Road 20706 (or whatever the No.)
FS112	U. S. Forest Service Road 112 (or whatever the No.)
T-307	Township Road 307 (or whatever the No.)
RR	Railroad (usually a long-abandoned logging grade)
N	north (northerly, etc.)
S	south (southerly, etc.)
E	east
W	west
NE	northeast, etc.
SSW	south-southwest, etc.
3.6mi	3.6 (or whatever the number) miles (1.0mi=1.61km)
4.3km	4.3 (or whatever the number) kilometers (1.km=0.62mi)
35ft	35 (or whatever the number) feet (used only with reference to vertical distances)
50yd	50 (or whatever the number) yards (1.0mi=1760yd)
2.3sq.mi	2.3 (or whatever the number) square miles (640 acres= 1.0sq.mi) (Areas under 64 acres (0.1sq.mi) are expressed in units of acres.)
topo	U.S.Geological Survey 7.5' topographic map
ORV	Off-road (motorized) vehicle
CC	Clear cut (a completely logged area)
OGM	Oil, Gas and Mineral
NCT	North Country Trail

Please become familiar with these abreviations.

The first line of Notes on each trail gives the trail name
and the total length of the trail in miles and kilometers.

The second line of Notes rates the trail according to
three attributes: Scenery (SCEN), Difficulty (DIFF) and trail
condition (COND). The definitions of these rating systems are
given below.

Scenery (SCEN:):
(1) Wild setting with exceptional scenic or natural appeal
    and/or points of particular interest such as scenic views,
    interesting geologic formations, waterfalls.
(2) Basically wooded setting and/or little noticeable civi-
    lization, but without points of particular interest.
(3) Mainly of a pastoral- or more developed nature (scenery
    influenced significantly by farms, unshaded logging roads,

One of many giant stumps in a meadow along Bear Creek, north of
Bear Creek Picnic Area.

recent clearcuts, proximity to highways, communications
towers, storage tanks, OGM operations, etc.)

Difficulty (DIFF:):

(I) Suitable for leisurely stroll. Ordinary low-heeled street
shoes are adequate.

(II) May involve moderate amounts of scrambling over rocks,
climbing steep slopes, etc. Good walking shoes are recommended.

(III) A reasonable amount of hiking experience and good phys-
ical condition are recommended as prerequisites. Hiking
boots or work boots are suggested.

Trail Condition (COND:):

(A) Well blazed and maintained. No difficulty in finding trail.
Few, if any, brambles, fallen logs or similar obstacles.

(B) Average. Trail can be followed if reasonably close attention is paid to blazes, maps, treadway, etc. Obstacles are
not so bad as to obscure the trail route.

(C) Poorly blazed and maintained; one may find difficulty in
finding and staying on the trail. Hikers are likely to
encounter brambles, fallen logs, washouts, and similar
obstacles.

The third line of Notes on each trail summarizes information tabulated in columns 5, 7, and 8 of the Table of Trails,
i.e.:

SKI-: Ski-Touring Rating from Column 5
NOTE: Special Notes from Col.5 (The number in parentheses
is the number of stream crossings from Column 8)
ELEV: Maximum elevation/Minimum elevation encountered on
the trail route (from Column 7)

The fourth line of each trail writeup lists maps that are
useful in following the trail. The map denoted by USFS(A) is
the Forest Recreation Map (1 inch= 2 miles). The 7.5' USGS
topographic map(s) (2.64 inches= 1 mile) pertinent to the trail
are also listed. See page 38 for more detailed information
about these maps, plus information on how to obtain these maps.
In most cases, relevant portions of these topo maps are repro-
duced in this Guide at the end of the appropriate chapter.
These maps are numbered according to the scheme shown on Map 5
on page 58 .

The fifth line of the Trail Notes begins a table of trail
segments and their lengths. Ends of segments are usually at
intersecting roads and trails or other readily identifiable
landmarks. The total length of all segments should equal the
trail length given on Line 1. Sometimes an additional trail
"segment" will be added in parentheses to the end of the list.
This segment is a part of some other trail that you need to
take to get to a road access.

The first paragraph of the Notes on a trail usually contains general information about the trail--information not specific to any particular point along the trail.

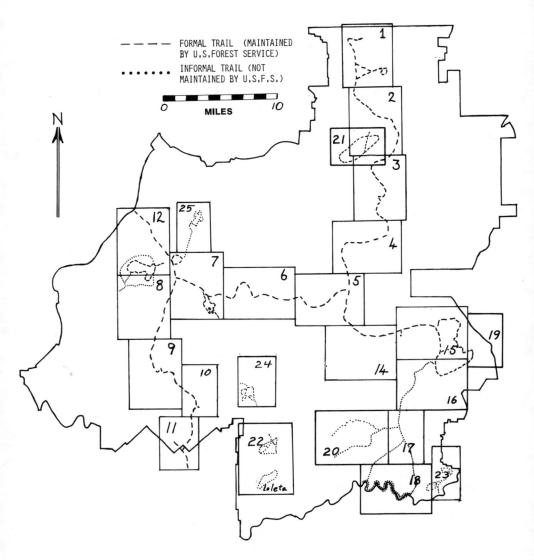

Legend:
- FORMAL TRAIL (MAINTAINED BY U.S.FOREST SERVICE)
- INFORMAL TRAIL (NOT MAINTAINED BY U.S.F.S.)

0 MILES 10

N

MAP 5 – KEY TO THE TOPOGRAPHIC MAPS IN THIS GUIDE

The next paragraph gives information on getting to the trailheads by car, car shuttles, trailheads, parking, signing, nearby camping opportunities, etc.--information you need before setting foot on the trail.

The paragraphs following the paragraph(s) on trailhead information give information needed to follow the trail, plus notes on specific attractions and problems to be encountered along the trail. Ideally, one paragraph is devoted to each trail segment listed in the table starting on Line 4 or 5.

Scene along Tracy Ridge Trail.

TABLE OF FOOT TRAILS

TRAIL NAME (SYMBOL)	START//FINISH	RANGER DISTRICT	LENGTH MILES(KM)
NORTHERN ALLEGHENY NATIONAL FOREST			
North Country (NCT0)	Willow Bay//Allegany State Pk.	B	1.2(1.9
North Country (NCT1)	Willow Bay//Sugar Bay	B	9.6(15.4
North Country (NCT2)	Sugar Bay(PA321)//Chappel Bay	B	12.5(20.1
North Country (NCT3)	Chappel Bay(PA321)//US6	B,R	12.2(19.6
Tracy Ridge (TRT)	PA321//PA321 (loop)	B	6.5(10.5
Land-of-Many-Uses (LMU)	T.R.Campground //(loop)	B	2.5(4.0
Rimrock-Morrison (RMT)	PA59 //PA59 (loop)	B	12.3(19.8
SOUTHWESTERN ALLEGHENY NATIONAL FOREST			
North Country (NCT6)	Henrys Mill//Minister Hill Rd.	S	11.1(17.9
North Country (NCT7)	Minister Hill Rd.//Dunham Sid.	S	5.1(8.2
North Country (NCT8)	Dunham Siding//Kellettville	S	11.6(18.7
North Country (NCT9)	Kellettville//Baker Trail	M	18.5(29.8
Minister Creek (MCLT)	PA666//PA666 (loop)	S	6.5(10.5
Tanbark (TBT)	NCT7//US62	S	8.1(13.0
Tom Run Loop (TRLT)	TBT//TBT	S	3.5(5.6
Heart's Content Scenic Area (HCSAT)	Picnic Area//Picnic Area	S	1.0(1.6
Hickory Cr. Loop (HCLT)	H.C.Campground// (loop)	S	11.5(18.5
Little Side Loop (LSLT)	HCLT//HCLT	S	3.9(6.3
Big Side Loop (BSLT)	HCLT//HCLT	S	11.2(18.0
Allegheny Front NRA	PA337//US62	S	- (-
Beaver Meadows (BMLT)	B.M.Campground// (loops)	M	6.8(10.9
SOUTHEASTERN ALLEGHENY NATIONAL FOREST			
North Country (NCT4)	US6//Tionesta Scenic Area	R,S	5.2(8.4
North Country (NCT5)	Tionesta S.A.//Henry's Mill	S	10.1(16.3
Twin Lakes (TLT)	Twin L.Rec.Area//NCT5	R	15.9(25.6
Black Cherry (BCT)	Twin L.Rec.Area// (loop)	R	1.6(2.6
Mill Creek Loop (MCL)	Twin L.Rec.Area// (loop)	R	16.7(26.9
Upper Bear Creek (UBCT)	MCLT//Bear Creek Picnic Area	R	10.2(16.4
Lower Bear Creek (LBCT)	Bear Creek Picnic Area//T-307	R	6.5(10.5
Clarion River (CRT)	T-307//IRT	R	9.3(15.0
Irwin Run (IRT)	CRT//(LBCT)	R	6.1(9.8
Big Run (BRT)	FS130//LBCT	R	7.4(11.9
Pigeon Run Falls (PRFT)	FS130//FS136(Owls Nest)	R	5.9(9.5
Laurel Mill Ski (LMST)	T-307//T-307 (loops)	R	11.0(17.7
Buzzard Swamp Ski (BSST)	FS157 and FS376 (loops)	M	7.6(12.2
Songbird Sojourn (SSIT)	FS157//FS157 (loop)	M	1.6(2.6
Loleta Hiking (LHT)	Loleta Campground// (loop)	M	3.0(4.8

NOTES	INTERSECTING TRAILS & ROADS	ELEVATION MAX./MIN.	STREAM CROSS.	PAGE NO.	MAPS
B,M,?	-	1910/1380	2	64	1
B,M,S4	TRT, JCT	1950/1330	5	64	1,2
B,M,S2	PA59	2110/1330	4	65	2,3
B,M,S4	PA321,Gibbs Hill Rd.	2050/1330	2	68	3,4
B,M,S2-4	Alleg. Res.,NCT,LMU	2250/1330	5	70	1
I,S2	TRT	2200/2070	0	73	1
B,M,S2	Allegheny Reservoir	2100/1360	8	73	21
B,M,S2	FS179,FS255	1950/1300	2	87	6,7
B,M,S2	FS419,MCLT,TBT	1850/1390	1	88	7
B,M,S4	FS449	1870/1170	11	89	7,8,9
B,M,S4	FS145,Muzette Road	1800/1170	5	91	9,10,11
B,M,S4	NCT7	1700/1240	5	93	7
B,M,S4	HCLT,TRLT,HCSAT,FS18/	1890/1060	2	95	7,12
B	HCLT,(HCSAT),TBT PA337	1910/1620	0	98	7,12
I,S2	TBT	1900/1800	0	98	12
B,M,S4	TBT	1950/1450	2	101	8,12
B,M,S2	BSLT	1700/1330	2	102	8,12
B,M,S4	LSLT	1840/1320	13	104	8,12
B,M,S4	TBT	1900/1080	-	105	12
M,S1-2	-	1770/1670	0	107	24
B,M,S4	FS133,FS149,Wetmore Rd.	1910/1480	0	136	4,5
B,M,S3	TLT,PA948	1970/1300	1	137	5,6
B,M,S4	MCL,BCT,FS31,PA66,FS152	2040/1450	7	139	5,14,15
M,I,S1	MCL,TLT	1850/1750	0	142	15
B,M,S4	TLT,(PA948),BCT,UBCT	2060/1630	6	142	15,16,19
B,M,S1	PA948	1910/1450	14	144	15,16,17
B,M,S4	T-307	1450/1320	4	149	17,18
B,M,S4	LBCT,Arroyo Bridge	1310/1290	2	150	18
B,M,S4	FS136	1750/1290	6	153	17,18,20
B,M,S4	FS136	1800/1330	6	154	17,20
B,M,S4	BRT	1800/1366	?	157	20
M,S1-2	-	1700/1400	0	158	23
M,S1-2	SSIT	1700/1600	0	159	22
I,M,S4	BSXT	1800/1700	0	160	22
M,S2	-	1600/1300	1	160	22

Fern carpet along North Country Trail northeast of Minister Creek Valley.

THE NORTH COUNTRY TRAIL

In 1968 Congress passed the National Trail System Act. Two trails were made initial components of the National Trail System and 14 trails were designated as possible future additions. The North Country Trail (NCT) was designated a National Scenic Trail in March, 1980, and is now a component of the National Trail System.

The NCT serves as the backbone of the established trail system in the ANF. From the N boundary of the ANF the NCT proceeds from Willow Bay into New York State's Allegany State Park and connects with the Finger Lakes Trail system. At the southern end of the ANF the NCT emerges from the Forest and joins the Baker Trail for some miles before turning W through Moraine State Park. Thus it links the Pittsburgh area with New York and the Bruce Trail in Canada. Eventually it may connect to the 70-mile Laurel Highlands Trail and, via the Potomac Heritage Trail or the Allegheny Trail, extend to West Virginia. The route of the trail is shown in Map 5.

The description of the trail in these Trail Notes is limited to the portion that lies in the ANF. An address (for maps) is provided below for those who want to hike the NCT in Allegany State Park (adjacent to the ANF on the N) N to Finger Lakes Trail. The Notes here start at the N terminus, near the New York border, on the E side of Allegheny (Kinzua) Reservoir, and follow the trail S and W to the Baker Trail. The NCT has been divided into ten sections, each beginning at a convenient access point.

		Section Miles	Cumulative Miles
0	Allegany State Park (NY) to Willow Bay	1.2	1.2
1	Willow Bay to Sugar Bay	10.6	11.8
2	Sugar Bay to Chappel Bay	11.8	23.6
3	Chappel Bay to US 6	11.7	35.3
4	US 6 to Tionesta Scenic Area	5.3	40.6
5	Tionesta Scenic Area to Henrys Mill	6.6	47.2
6	Henrys Mill to Minister Hill Road	8.7	55.9
7	Minister Hill Road to Dunham Siding	5.0	60.9
8	Dunham Siding to Kellettville	11.5	72.4
9	Kellettville to the Baker Trail	15.6	88.0

The mileages quoted above are from the USFS (1/90). Mileage figures in the Notes below were obtained from one of the following sources:

- running a bicycle wheel over the trails during the process of scouting trails for this Guide (This was done by Carolyn Weilacher Yartz and friends, mainly in the SE ANF.),
- running a map-measuring wheel over the trail route on 7.5' USGS topographic maps and multiplying by a "wiggle-factor" correction of 1.10.

TRAILS OF NORTHERN ALLEGHENY
NATIONAL FOREST

NCT SECTION 0: WILLOW BAY TO ALLEGANY STATE PARK   1.2mi(1.9km)
SCEN: ?   DIFF: ?   COND: ?
SKI : ?   NOTE: B,M,2   ELEV: 1910/1380
MAPS: Cornplanter Run, USFS(A), Map 1 in this Guide
TRAIL SEGMENTS:
 (1) Willow Bay (PA346) to New York Line   1.2mi

    Scouting reports are not available for this trail segment
which runs up Schoolhouse Hollow from Willow Bay ⃞A. The NCT
extends into Allegany State Park (N.Y.) and on to the Finger
Lakes Trail System. To obtain a map of the NCT in Allegany
State Park, write to Allegany State Park, R.D.1, Salamanca, NY
14779 (716-354-2545).

NCT SECTION 1: WILLOW BAY TO SUGAR BAY   9.6mi(15.4km)
SCEN: 1-2   DIFF: II   COND: B
SKI : S4   NOTE: B,M,5   ELEV: 1950/1330
MAPS: Cornplanter Run, USFS(A), Maps 1 and 2 in this Guide
TRAIL SEGMENTS:
 (1) Willow Bay (PA346) to Tracy Ridge Trail   3.6mi
 (2) Tracy Ridge Trail to Johnnycake Trail   2.2mi
 (3) Johnnycake Trail to Handsome Lake Campground 1.1mi
 (4) Handsome Lake Campground to Sugar Bay (PA321) 2.7mi

    The main attractions of this section of the NCT are views
of Allegheny Reservoir and several campgrounds, some accessible
only by boat or on foot. This is a wild and wooded section of
the NCT, and even though Segments 1, 2 and 3 closely parallel
Allegheny (Kinzua) Reservoir, you seldom get uninterrupted
views of the water during the summer. However there are many
places where you can leave the trail and drop down to the
water's edge for the views or a swim. Several spots along the
trail can be soft and muddy in the spring and during rainy
periods when the streams are full. Moderate scrambling and
some steep slopes are encountered, so good walking shoes are
recommended. Drinking water is available at Handsome Lake and
Hopewell Campgrounds.
Access: Parking at the N trailhead is possible for 6-8 vehicles along the N side of PA346. For information on the S
trailhead, see the description of NCT Section 2 below.
Segment (1): Starting from Willow Bay, the white blazes of NCT
start on the S side of PA346 at the bridge over Willow Creek (
⃞A, Map 1). At the top of a short climb the NCT meets a side
trail (shown on Map 1) leading NW to Willow Bay Campground
(labeled "Willow Bay Recreation Area" on Map 1). Climb gradu-

ally W, then turn S and pass through the westernmost saddle in the ridge [C]. Descend S towards Allegheny Reservoir, with old logging road traces and small stream crossings. Head SE to North Branch [E] and briefly follow an old road downstream until you cross North Branch and Tracy Run. Bear W around the bay after Tracy Run, meeting Tracy Ridge Trail [G] descending from Tracy Ridge Campground and PA321.

Segment (2): Continue S along the steep hillside strewn with large boulders. Allegheny Reservoir is visible below, but only as glimpses through the trees. Cross Whiskey Run [I] filled with large boulders. Some moderate rock blocks are seen in the woods. Pass along the E edge of the old clearing shown on the topo, with planted pines. Proceed SE across several ravines, and intersect Johnnycake Trail [K] coming down from Tracy Ridge, before crossing Johnnycake Run.

Segment (3): The trail turns sharply W 0.4mi along the S edge of Johnnycake Run and then turns S at the Reservoir for a short distance. Turn SE and cross an unnamed run. A right turn downstream will quickly lead to the old hardtop road which provides access to Handsome Lake Campground on the reservoir.

Segment (4): The trail then climbs through nice hemlocks and out of the stream valley along an old wood road shown on topo. Watch closely for the blue-blazed marker that marks the turn S 0.7mi down the road leading to Hopewell Campground (shown on Map 2). Beyond the 1800' crest by 20yd turn E up a spur ridge [M]. Walk SE along the spur ridge and pass over a saddle ([O], Map 2). Drop down into a side stream valley of Nelse Run. Pick up a grassy logging road on the S bank of stream, and continue your descent through some nice hemlock and pine. On reaching Nelse Run [Q] turn E across Nelse Run just short of Allegheny Reservoir, then head NE away from Nelse Run and climb up a spur trail to PA321 [S].

NCT SECTION 2: SUGAR BAY TO CHAPPEL BAY   12.5mi(20.1km)

SCEN: 1-2   DIFF: II   COND: B
SKI-: S2   NOTE: B,M,4   ELEV: 2110/1330
MAPS: Cornplanter Run, Stickney, Westline, Cornplanter Bridge,
      USFS(A), Maps 2 and 3 in this Guide
TRAIL SEGMENTS:
  (1) Sugar Bay (PA321) to Hammond Run   2.4mi
  (2) Hammond Run to PA59   3.3mi
  (3) PA59   to Chappel Bay (PA321)   6.8mi

    This section of NCT travels through pleasant woodlands and closely parallels two major runs, but there are no views or major attractions.

Access: To get to the N trailhead, watch for a trail sign on the W side of PA321 [S], 0.6 mi W and N of North Branch [U] of Sugar Run. Cars (6-8) can park in a small lot just off the berm. A spur trail leads downhill 30 yds. NW to the main NCT.

There is also unlimited parking available along an old road leading down along the N bank of Sugar Run to the point where Sugar Run and North Branch empty into Sugar Bay.

At the intermediate access point, PA59, ($\boxed{H}$, Map 2) cars may be parked on Hemlock Trail. This point is 2.4mi W of the USFS ranger station at the junction of PA59 and PA321. It is also 5.3mi E of Cornplanter Bridge. For information on the Chappel Bay (PA321) trailhead access, see the description of NCT Section 3 below. Access to the NCT from PA321 is also available at the junction of Sugar Run and Hammond Run $\boxed{Y}$.

Segment (1): Starting from the N $\boxed{S}$, follow the shoreline of Sugar Bay through open woods until the NCT climbs up to PA321. ($\boxed{U}$, Map 2). A trail sign can be seen from the trail and from PA321 at this point. Follow the highway guard rail across North Branch of Sugar Run. Leave PA321 and head S through a marshy area and across an old highway towards Sugar Run $\boxed{W}$, then SE along Sugar Run to a new bridge across the run. Follow Sugar Run on its S bank to Hammond Run $\boxed{Y}$. Some large hem-locks, ferns and tall grass are found along the trail.

Segment (2): The NCT starts up the W bank of Hammond Run on an open, grassy logging road that angles gradually uphill (S). Watch for a turn to left (NE) off the grassy path $\boxed{Z}$. From here on the NCT runs through scenic, open woods, close to the Hammond Run stream bed. The water looks clear, and numerous sites for small-group, primitive camping are found here. (Camp only above the 1600-ft. contour.) Cross Hammond Run $\boxed{B}$ and head N. Eventually, near a dirt road (not shown on the topo), the trail switch-backs E up to the crest of a small ridge $\boxed{D}$, passing a giant hemlock. Follow this ridge line S to "Hemlock Trail", a dirt road in good condition $\boxed{F}$. Proceed W along Hemlock Trail to where it comes within 10yd of PA59. The NCT crosses PA59 here at a point marked by a trail sign $\boxed{H}$.

Segment (3): The trail leaves PA59 through a broad meadow with scattered trees and large expanses of ferns. Abandoned build-ings (and machinery), shown on the topo 0.4mi below PA59, can be seen through the trees (interesting side trip). The trail crosses a dirt road (not shown on the topo). Continue through a broad meadow with scattered trees and large expanses of fern for 0.5mi before descending into the Hemlock Run Valley. The trail crosses this attractive stream and stays close to it through open woods, "deep and dark"--no views but very pleas-ant. The trail occasionally follows an old RR grade. Near Chappel Bay a clearcut can be seen through the trees on the W side of Hemlock Run. No other works of man are evident. Prim-itive camping for small groups is possible at numerous spots along Hemlock Run. At Chappel Bay ($\boxed{K}$, Map 3) (Chappel Fork of Kinzua Creek) follow the shoreline E to emerge, via a dirt road, onto PA321 $\boxed{M}$. Turn right (W) and follow the trail close to PA321 for 0.4mi to the trailhead $\boxed{O}$. Note the short-cut, shown on the topo, useable in periods of low water.

Aerial view of Allegheny Front Area (far side of Allegheny River). Photo courtesy U.S. Forest Service.

NCT SECTION 3:   CHAPPEL BAY TO US6   12.2mi(19.6km)
SCEN: 1-2   DIFF: II   COND: A
SKI-: S4   NOTE: B,M,2   ELEV: 2050/1330
MAPS: Cornplanter Bridge, Westline, Ludlow, Kane, USFS(A),
      Maps 3 and 4 in this Guide
TRAIL SEGMENTS:
  (1) Chappel Bay   to Red Bridge (PA321)   4.3mi
  (2) Red Bridge (PA321) to Gibbs Hill Road   3.1mi
  (3) Gibbs Hill Road   to US6   4.8mi

     This is a wild and wooded section of the NCT that involves
moderate-to-steep climbs and nice views. The forest is mixed
hardwood with many stands of pine. Drinking water is available
only at Red Bridge Campground, which involves leaving the trail
at PA321 and back-tracking a bit. Many good sites for primitive camping are found near the trail. The trail itself is in
good condition and newly blazed in 1989. Stream-crossings are
small and seasonal.
Access: To get to the N trailhead ([O],Map 3), watch for the
trail sign on the S side of PA321 near Chappel Bay (Chappel
Fork of Kinzua Creek), just E of the powerline crossing. This
point is 5.5mi SW of the Bradford Ranger Station at the junction of PA59 and PA321. It is also 4.8mi N of the intersection
of PA321 and Longhouse Scenic Drive (FS262). Parking space is
very limited in the immediate area. Cars can park on the dirt
road 0.4mi further E on the N side of PA321 ([M],Map 3).
     At the intermediate (Red Bridge) access, parking can be
found between [W] and Red Bridge Campground N on PA321. Cars
can also park on a black-top access road leading down to a boat
ramp on the S end of Red Bridge on the W side of PA321. No
parking is available where the NCT crosses FS262. Parking is
possible at the Gibbs Hill Road trailhead [C] on a wide, grassy
shoulder.
     The S trailhead offers parking for 8-10 cars on the S side
of US6. The NCT sign here is on the N side of US6. This point
is 1.7mi E of Gibbs Hill Road and 7.8mi E of the Sheffield
Ranger Station or 6.6mi W of Kane.
Segment (1): Starting from Chappel Bay [O], follow a grassy
road ESE for 100yd, then proceed uphill along a ravine. Cross
three dirt roads and continue to climb. Reach a hill top [Q]
amid old wood roads and nice hemlocks. Pass a clearcut and
cross a new dirt road. Turn S and cross the upper branch of
Root Run [S]. Follow downstream along a woods road, with an
attractive stream bottom on the right (N). Cross Root Run and
continue along the N bank past several openings suitable for
primitive camping. Where the valley widens, climb to 1600' [U]
and stay on the contour (crossing FS667) until you find yourself turning NW. Then follow FS122 as it drops down to PA321
[W], 0.2mi S of Red Bridge Campground. A trail sign here on
the W side of PA321 points back the way you came. Follow PA321
S over Red Bridge over Kinzua Creek. Good campsites don't

exist between Red Bridge and US6. The next good campsites are
1.8 to 2.5mi S of US6.

Segment (2): The NCT goes right (SW) into the woods [Y] where
PA321 turns off to a boat ramp. No sign marks this spot. Soon
cross FS262 which is signed. Just S of FS262 is a dedication
marker: "Allegheny Outdoor Club 1974". Begin climbing steadily
uphill above a road past large blocks of rock. Then climb
steeply toward the ridge top, and join a good road running NE
along the ridge. Reach a fine viewpoint [A] at the end of this
ridge and then double back (S) over the summit. Follow the
hillside W, crossing small ravines, before reaching an old RR
grade. After 0.4mi, turn left (E) and proceed steeply downhill, cross a stream, and climb to paved Gibbs Hill Road [C]
where the NCT is signed. There is supposed to be a dedication
marker just before Gibbs Hill Road.

Segment (3): Cross Gibbs Hill Road and climb 22 steps up the
bank. Continue up to the ridge top [E] with a large clearcut
below, providing good views. Cross the end of the ridge, and
head almost due S at the USFS boundary markers. With a logging
road and clearcut below, good views are available across the
valley of the South Branch of Kinzua Creek valley on the left
(E). The NCT eventually leads into level, open woods. (See
Map 4.) Cross a good woods road, continue along the flat ridge
top, and cross another good woods road. Encounter old oil
pipes and flat woods, then pine woods and old wood roads. Turn
W, gradually dropping. Cross minor streams. Pass a gas well
site. Drop off the hill to US6 [G].

TRACY RIDGE AND TRACY RIDGE TRAIL

Tracy Ridge Trail traverses the 15.6 sq.mi Tracy Ridge
area near the New York State line. Extending for 6.5mi along
the E bank of Allegheny Reservoir, Tracy Ridge is bounded on
the S by Sugar Bay and on the N by Willow Bay. It is one of
the largest relatively undisturbed areas in the ANF. Elevations range from 2245 feet on the level ridge tops near Tracy
Ridge Campground to the 1328 foot normal pool elevation of
Allegheny Reservoir. Slopes along the reservoir and along the
small streams which drain the area are steep. Nice rock ledges
are found W of Tracy Ridge Campground, and large boulders are
found on the steeper hillsides.

Most of the region is heavily forested in second growth
timber; largely oak, mixed with beech, black cherry, and hickory. Hemlock are found in pleasing groves along the streams,
and some magnificent old white pines are found in scattered
locations. Wildlife, including deer, squirrel, grouse, and
wild turkey, is plentiful; black bear are relatively numerous
and large for Pennsylvania. A heron rookery is located in the
area.

The region is rich in history, due to its location along a
major transportation route--Allegheny River. Several Indian

villages were nearby; the Indians hunted here and artifacts are often found. White settlement along the river began in 1827 and before 1900 the original pine-hemlock forest was logged. Most of the land was not suited for farming, and was taken into the National Forest when established in 1923. Several remaining private tracts were acquired when Kinzua Dam was completed in 1966 to form the Allegheny Reservoir. One peripheral 160-acre tract remains in private hands.

Within the last decade some selective cutting and some clearcutting has occurred around the periphery. There was oil and gas activity with limited success in the 1890's, again in the 1940's, and recently around the periphery. No wells are active, and the old sites represent rather minor disturbances of the natural setting. Mineral rights for most of the area are not in public ownership and opinions differ regarding prospects for future oil and gas activity. An unused pipeline crosses the extreme S end of the area.

Four campgrounds are on the periphery of the area; two have access only by boat or on foot. Willow Bay Campground (70 units) on the N end is 15mi W of Bradford along PA346. Not far N from there, along PA346, is the Quaker Area of Allegany State Park. Tracy Ridge Campground (120 large, tree-shaded units) on the E edge of Tracy Ridge is also accessible by car. (Water at Tracy Ridge Campground is reputed to have an odor and high mineral content.)

Tracy Ridge (Run) Trail begin near Tracy Ridge Campground. Using a 2.2mi section of the NCT, it forms a triangular loop that makes a pleasant 9.8mi hike from PA321 and back, with camping opportunities on the shores of Allegheny Reservoir. An interpretive trail ("Land of Many Uses") circles Tracy Ridge Campground. The S leg of Tracy Ridge (Run) Trail was called Johnnycake Trail before 1990.

TRACY RIDGE TRAIL   6.5mi(10.5km)
SCEN: 1-2   DIFF: II   COND: A
SKI-: S2-S4   NOTE: B,M,5   ELEV: 2250/1330
MAPS: Cornplanter Run, Stickney, USFS(A), Map 1 in this Guide
TRAIL SEGMENTS:
  (1) PA321 to S branch of Tracy Ridge Trail   1.1mi
  (2) S branch (via N branch) to NCT & Allegheny Res. 3.0mi
       (via NCT S to S branch of Tracy Ridge Trail   2.2mi)
  (3) NCT to N branch of Tracy Ridge Trail   2.4mi
       (Then return to the trailhead via Segment (1)   1.1mi)

A general description of Tracy Ridge area is given above. Nice views of the small bay and of Allegheny Reservoir are found at the junction of Tracy Ridge Trail and the NCT. The first 3.0mi of Tracy Ridge Trail run along the level ridge and go through mixed hardwoods including red oak and maple. Some interesting large blocks of rock are found along the trail.

The trail is usually dry. Trail use is heavy on weekends.
There are many places to camp along the trail. Remember to
camp at least 70yd from roads or the reservoir and 30yd off the
trail. These rules are enforced, especially when use is heavy.
The trail is blazed with blue "i" blazes. The trail has been
designated as a National Recreation Trail. The only other so-
designated trail in the ANF is the Black Cherry Interpretive
loop Trail near Twin Lakes.
Access: The E trailhead is 0.25mi N of the well-marked entrance to Tracy Ridge Campground at the N end of an open field
on PA321 ($\boxed{S}$, Map 1). Note the trail sign at the gated dirt
road. Parking is available for 10-15 cars. This trailhead is
11.mi N of the junction of PA59 and PA321. It is also 2.8mi S
of the junction of PA346 and PA321.
     Tracy Ridge (Run) Trail may also be reached (old route)
from the back of the campground, on a woods road descending
from the rear of the first campground loop (between Campsites
11 and 12). For this latter route, make the first right turn
(W) after the left turn (S) of the main entrance road to the
campground.
     The W trailhead is accessible only by boat (Allegheny
Reservoir) or by foot (NCT).
Segment (1): Starting from PA321 $\boxed{S}$ follow the grassy road W
to the back of the open field (Johnson Farm) marked on the
topo. Watch carefully for the alert blaze or a trail sign
marking a left turn off the grassy road. The trail follows the
edge of a flat hilltop (SW), gradually entering the woods.
After 0.2mi you encounter the "Land-of-Many-Uses" Interpretive
Trail (green-blazed) which follows the same route as Tracy
Ridge Trail for the next 0.9mi (to $\boxed{U}$). Crossing through an
area of large rocks, Tracy Ridge Trail bears W with the campground entry road to the left (S). The trail continues W with
the campground to the S and an interesting area of rock ledges
to the N. Emerge on and join a woods road leading down from
the campground (the alternative (former) access route). More
rock ledges are found to the S.
Segment (2): The S leg of Tracy Ridge Trail and "Land-of-Many-
Uses" Trail branch off to the left (S) at a clearing (old
(1943) OGM site with a concrete pad and settling pond) $\boxed{U}$.
The N leg of Tracy Ridge Trail stays level on the high ridge,
through oak and maple, with hickory near the end. At the end
of the ridge pass along a saddle $\boxed{W}$ and bear NW along a second
ridge. Then drop steeply off the end of the ridge down to the
NCT at the Allegheny Reservoir $\boxed{G}$, passing through maple and
beech, and finally large hemlock and beech. Just S of the
Tracy Ridge Trail junction with the NCT is a pleasant lunch
spot on the shore of Allegheny Reservoir. A blaze near the end
of the steep climb (for those heading in the opposite direction) could be confusing.
     Turn left (S) and follow the NCT (Section 1) 2.2mi to the
S leg of Tracy Ridge Trail (formerly Johnnycake Trail) $\boxed{K}$.

Aerial view of Tracy Ridge Area from the north. Willow Bay in foreground, Allegheny (Kinzua) Reservoir on right. Photo courtesy U.S. Forest Service.

(Just a little further S along NCT are a nice sandy beach and
good views, and 0.5mi further S along NCT is Handsome Lake
Campground for backpacker- and boat access only.)
Segment (3): Turn E up Johnnycake Run. The valley slopes here
are dominated by white oak with grass, ferns and patches of
pine. A few good campsites are available. Further up the valley the woods become quite open, with large trees, clearings,
wildlife, old apple trees and the foundation stones of an old
building. After crossing Johnnycake Run about five times, the
top of the plateau is reached. From the junction U with the
N leg of Tracy Ridge Trail follow Segment (1) back to the
trailhead and PA321.

LAND OF MANY USES INTERPRETIVE TRAIL   2.5mi(4.0km)
SCEN: 2   DIFF: I   COND: A
SKI-: S2   NOTE: 0   ELEV: 2200/2070
MAPS: Cornplanter Run, Stickney, USFS(A), Map 1 in this Guide
(The route is not shown on Map 1.)
TRAIL SEGMENTS:
 (1) Tracy Ridge Campground access road to same   2.5mi

     This green-blazed trail makes a loop around Tracy Ridge
Campground. It is meant for leisurely walks (1.5-2 hours) with
frequent stops at interpretive stations (marked with white numbers). It uses 0.9mi of Tracy Ridge Trail. It is so easy to
follow that no need is seen for a detailed description of the
route here. Hiking boots are recommended since there are some
rocky areas. The trail passes through two wildlife clearings
and an area of large blocks of rock where Indian artifacts have
been found.
Access: The trail begins along the road into Tracy Ridge Campground, 0.2mi W from PA321 and 0.5mi E of the campground information station. Parking is available for 5-6 cars. One could
also use the trailhead for Tracy Ridge (Run) Trail since the
two trails follow the same route for 0.9mi.

RIMROCK-MORRISON TRAIL   12.3mi(19.8km)
SCEN: 1-2   DIFF: II   COND: B
SKI-: S2   NOTE: B,M,8   ELEV: 2100/1360
MAPS: Cornplanter Bridge, USFS(A), Map 21 in this Guide
TRAIL SEGMENTS:
 (1) Perimeter Loop (W) to Morrison Campground   5.0mi
 (2) Perimeter Loop (E) to Morrison Campground   6.0mi
 (3) W Branch, Morrison Run Cross Trail   1.3mi
      (Southwest Loop   8.8mi)
      (East Loop   5.8mi)

     This double-loop trail is blazed with blue "i" blazes.
The terrain is generally steep. Wildlife (including bear) is

73

seen frequently in the area. The trail offers nice views of
Allegheny Reservoir, waterfalls, small meadows, large areas of
blueberries, and interesting large rock formations. In the
spring, wildflowers are found all along the route. In June
mountain laurel bloom in many areas along the trail. Telephone
inquiries about trail conditions should be directed to Bradford
Ranger District (814-362-4613). The trail is reported (1989)
to be heavily used.

Access: The main trail access ([A] , Map 21) is on PA59, 3.3mi
E of Cornplanter Bridge, 0.8mi E of Rimrock entrance road [B]
and 4.4mi W of PA321. Parking is available for 20 cars at this
trailhead. The trail is also accessible by boat at Morrison
Campground on Allegheny Reservoir. Other informal access
points exist, as Map 21 suggests. Several short, unmarked side
trails lead N to FS454 which goes from PA59 to Rimrock Overlook. (See below.)

Segment (1): About 0.5mi S of PA59 and 300yd W along the main
loop [D] the trail branches into three trails that allow you to
choose from 3 possible loops. The W branch goes to Campbell
Run and is the least interesting portion of the trail until it
nears Allegheny Reservoir. CAUTION: Along that route is a
dark-blue-blazed, signed trail leading W to FS454 and the Rimrock Picnic Area. To stay on the main trail make a sharp left
to the SW. About 0.8mi before the side trail leading down to
Morrison Campground (backpacker- and boat access only) are some
nice views of Allegheny Reservoir. At Morrison Campground are
picnic tables, a hand pump, fire rings, vault toilets and a
small beach. Even though it is not accessible to cars, it
often gets heavy use.

Segment 2: The E branch from [D] , the trail down Morrison Run,
is scenic, with lots of Hemlock and large hardwoods. The trail
up lower Morrison Run and its main tributary is reminiscent of
Minister Valley. Mountain Laurel is abundant, giving a late-
June visit an extra bonus. Generally, the trail up Morrison
Run's main tributary ([F] to [H]) is considered to be the best
segment of the trail system.

Segment 3: The middle (S) branch from [D] leading down the W
Branch of Morrison Run to [F] is particularly pleasant with
man-sized boulders, rock formations and small waterfalls. The
trail winds among these. This branch crosses the stream several times but this presents no problems. A good campsite is
found 30yd W of the trail near its N end.

POINTS OF INTEREST FOR HIKERS IN NORTHERN ALLEGHENY NATIONAL FOREST

Dewdrop Run

Driving on the Longhouse Scenic Drive (FS262) from PA59 to
PA321 along the W shore of Kinzua Bay takes you past the steep-
sided, narrow valley of Dewdrop Run. A 1.5mi trail winds up

this valley which is full of waterfalls, rapids, giant moss-covered boulders and dense woods. It is worth a visit. Near the mouth of Dewdrop Run is Dewdrop Campground and boat launch.

Dewdrop Campground

The Dewdrop Recreation Area is on the W shore of Kinzua Bay, a southern branch of Allegheny Reservoir, on Longhouse Scenic Drive (FS262) 4.mi S of PA59 at the W end of Cornplanter Bridge. It is also 16mi NW of Kane via PA321 and FS262. The campground has 74 large, shaded campsites, each with a table, fire ring and tent pad. The campground has water, flush toilets, hot showers and a boat launch ramp. The nearest beach is at Kinzua Beach along PA59 at the E end of Cornplanter Bridge.

Campbell Mill Interpretive Trail

This 2.0mi loop trail starts in Dewdrop Campground near the water's edge between Campsites 12 and 13. Trail guides can be obtained at the campground or at the Kinzua Point Information Center (KPIC) on PA59 just W of Cornplanter Bridge.

The trail is kept in a natural condition. Some sections are steep and have poor footing so hiking boots should be worn. The blue blazes are a bit confusing at the start. Follow the shoreline S 100yd and cross Dewdrop Run. Then follow it S and W until it crosses FS262. Along the trail are a number of interesting geological formations, a clear rushing stream, and large fern fields typical of the ANF.

Jake's Rocks Picnic Area and Overlook

Jake's Rocks Picnic Area and Overlook are reached from PA59 by turning S at the W end of Cornplanter Bridge onto FS262 (Longhouse Scenic Drive). Then turn right off FS262 0.5mi S of PA59 and drive about 2mi. The three main automobile overlooks and two walk-in overlooks gives excellent views of Allegheny Reservoir and Kinzua Dam. Indian Cave Trail leads to the base of the rocks. The shaded picnic area offers vault toilets, drinking water, tables and grills. The USFS offers a map of the trails, overlooks and other facilities in the area. (See page 25.)

Rimrock Overlook (See Map 21)

Rimrock Overlook offers a spectacular view of Kinzua Bay, the lower, E arm of Allegheny Reservoir. It is located off PA59, 2.6mi E of Cornplanter Bridge. Signs there direct you up a black-topped road (FS454). Paved walking trails lead to the rock edge. A natural stone stairway leads to the base of the rocks where one can explore. Springs flow from beneath the rocks.

Kiasutha Recreation Area

This area is located on FS262 (Longhouse Scenic Drive) 10mi S of the W end of Cornplanter Bridge on PA59 E of Warren.

It is also 10mi NW of Kane via PA321 and FS262. The facilities
lie along the W shore of Kinzua Bay, a southern branch of Allegheny Reservoir. It has a boat launch ramp, a large grassy
swimming beach, a bath house with hot showers, 90 large, shaded
campsites, flush toilets and a very nice picnic area.

Longhouse Interpretive Trail
This trail start at the W parking area of the boat launch
ramp in the Kiasutha Recreation Area. The trailhead is well
marked and interpretive guides are usually available. The
trail is 2.5mi long and well marked with double blue blazes.
It is kept in the most natural condition possible. Some portions are steep and have poor footing so hiking boots should be
worn.
About 100yd from its start the trail crosses FS262 and
begins a gradual ascent, passing through a mixed hardwood forest that is carpeted with at least five varieties of ferns.
Near the top of the 600ft. rise and about a mile from the
start, the forest becomes very dense and blackberry brambles
become a bother for 70yd. Some parts of the trail follow a
game trail and are steep and narrow. On the descent the forest
opens up considerably. The trail again crosses FS262. The
final 0.8mi is fairly level, passing through a mixed hardwood
forest plus lots of Eastern Hemlock.

Scene along Dewdrop Run.   Photo by John McNavage.

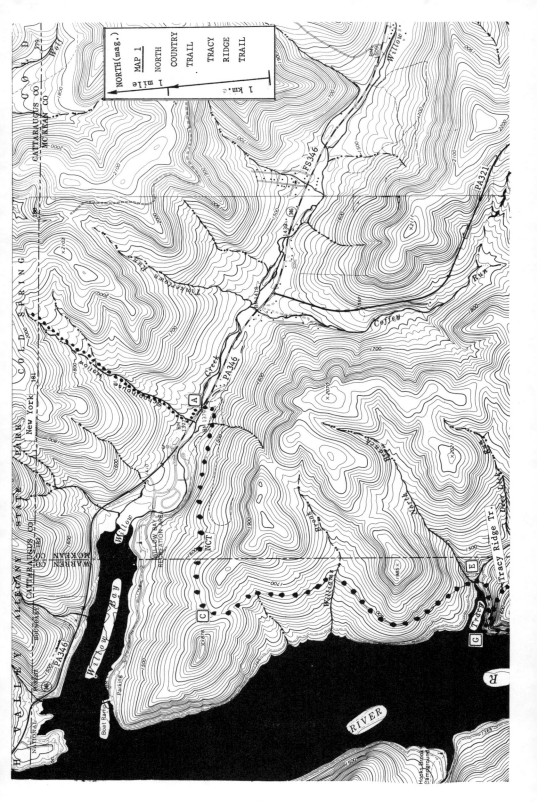

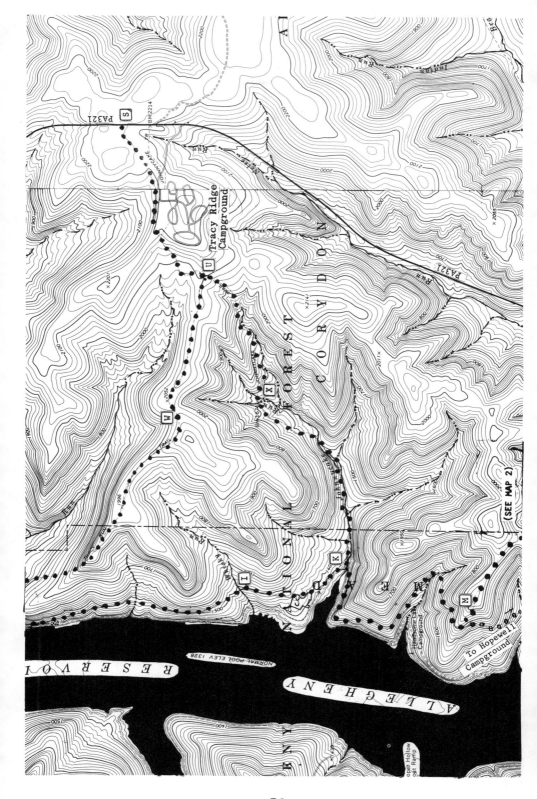

Tracy Ridge Campground

NATIONAL FOREST CORYDON

RESERVOIR

ALLEGHENY

NORMAL POOL ELEV 1328

To Hopewell Campground

(SEE MAP 2)

PA321

BM2214

PA321

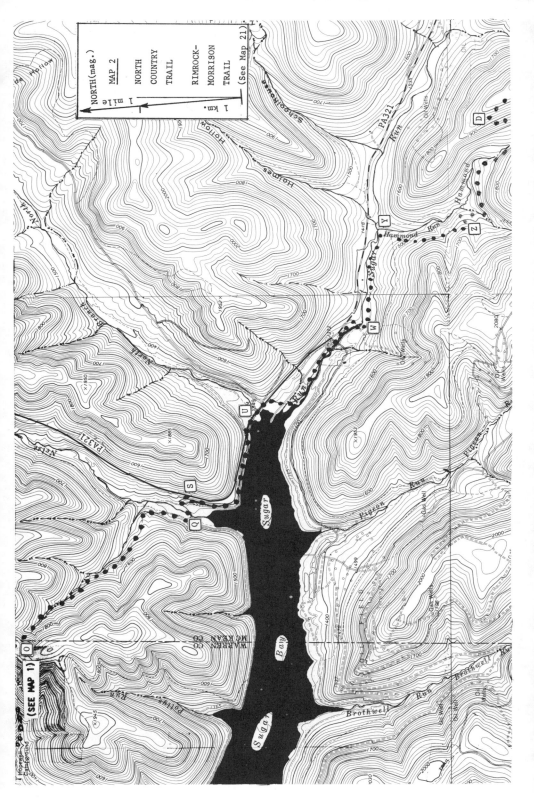

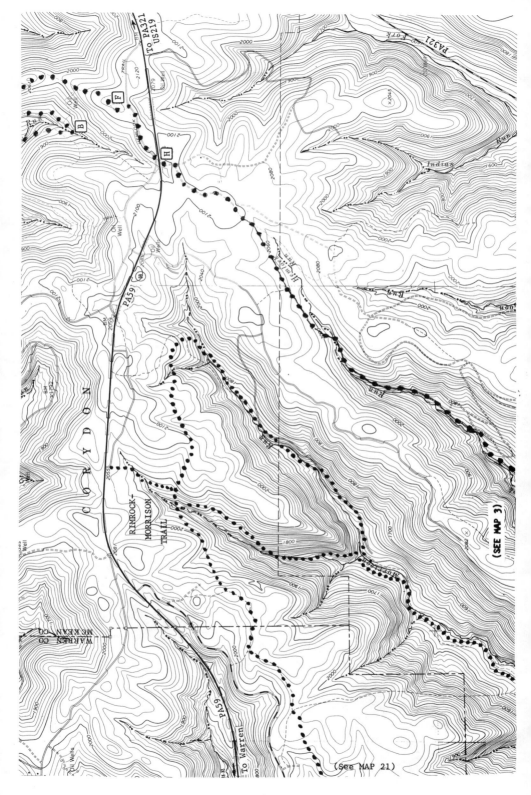

(SEE MAP 3)

(See MAP 21)

81

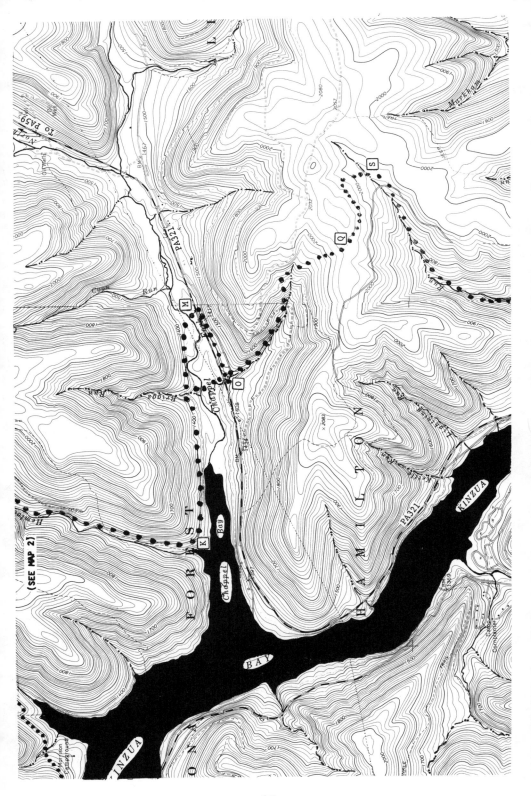

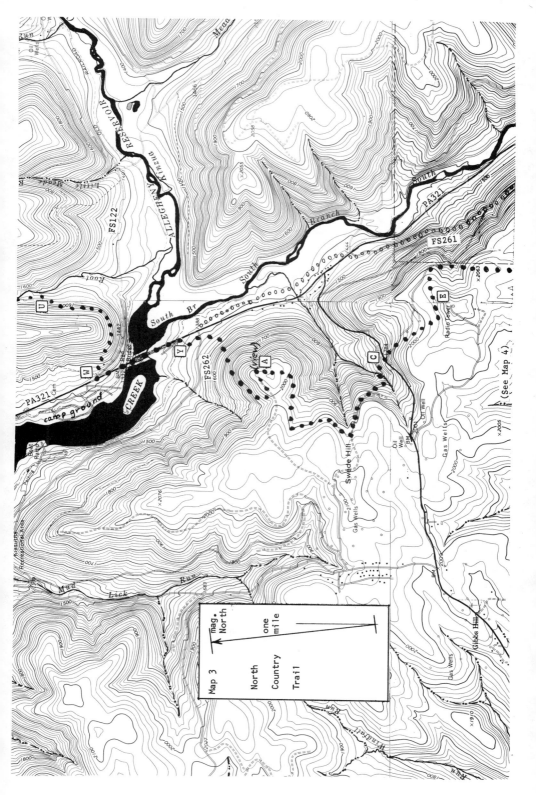

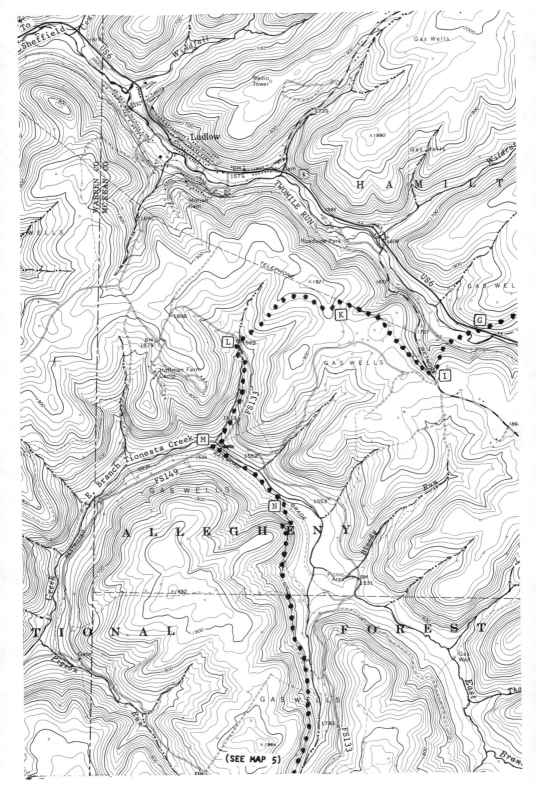

(SEE MAP 5)

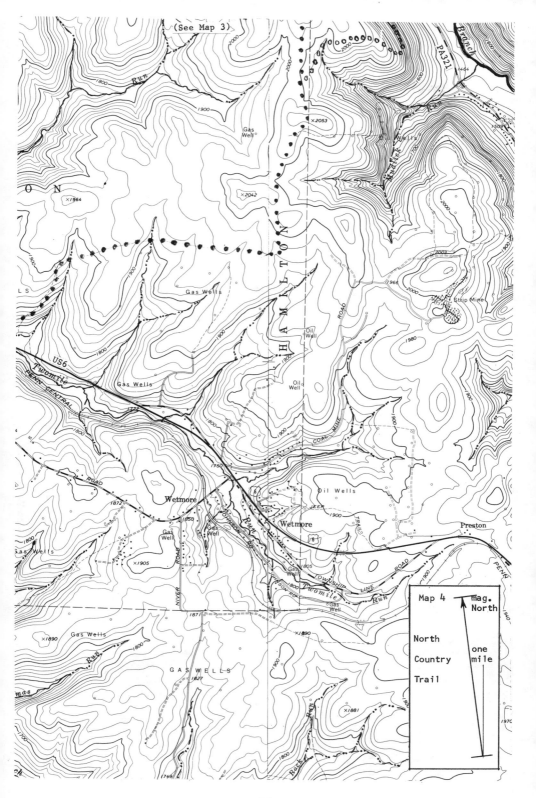

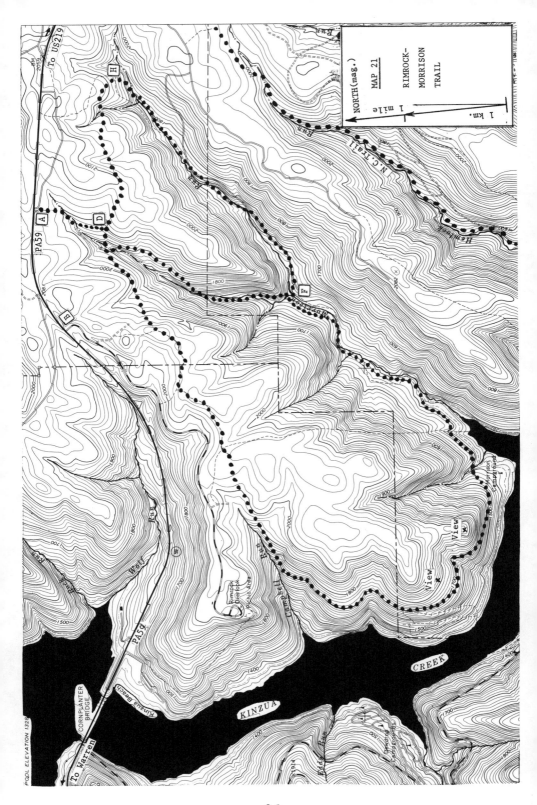

TRAILS OF SOUTHWESTERN ALLEGHENY

NATIONAL FOREST

NCT SECT. 6: HENRY'S MILLS TO MINISTER HILL ROAD 11.1mi(17.9km)
SCEN: 3   DIFF: I-II   COND: A
SKI-: S4   NOTE: B,M,5   ELEV: 1950/1300
MAPS: Sheffield, Cherry Grove, USFS(A), Maps 6 and 7 in this
      Guide
TRAIL SEGMENTS:
 (1) Henry's Mill to FS179   7.8mi
 (2) FS179 to FS255   2.4mi
 (3) FS255 to Minister Hill Road   0.9mi

Access: The E trailhead is at Henry's Mills on the N bank of
Tionesta Creek. The NCT crosses Tionesta Creek on the PA666
bridge ([A] ,Map 6). There is room to park cars near the S end
of the bridge. The foot trail resumes 300yd S of the PA666
bridge, just before PA666 crosses Messenger Run. There is also
a gated OGM road at this trailhead. There is room for 2-3 cars
at this gate without blocking the gate. The trail crossing of
FS179 is marked by a trail sign. However FS179 is gated at the
main road [R] . This crossing is 0.7mi S of the paved SR61031
leading E to Sheffield and PA948. (The ANF map erroneously
labels PA948 between Sheffield and Barnes as PA666.) Cars can
also park along FS255. The W trailhead is on Minister Hill
Road ([W] ,Map 7). A trail sign there reads "Henrys Mills 9mi"
but the actual distance is over 11mi.

Segment 1: Starting from the E, the NCT bears sharply WNW up
the hill overlooking the PA666 bridge. Reach grade and double
back SE around the hill side above the PA666 bridge. Head W
high on the N side of Messenger Run Valley. Other grades exist
up and down the hillside. A jeep road, marked on the topo, can
be seen in the valley. The trail stays on old unused roads,
old RR grades and pipelines through OGM sites. The trail gets
closer to the stream in Messenger Run, and changes to a newer
road as it enters a meadow [C] along the creek. Revert to the
old OGM roads and head NW through an oil well area to a saddle
[E] .

Descend NNW into the upper reaches of Pell Run Valley with
good views. Join a RR grade. A number of small stream crossings and stagnant pools are seen where the grade has formed
dams. Pass a well site [G] shown on the topo, and leave the RR
grade. Cross scenic Pell Run and climb up to meet another RR
grade. Turn W onto this grade and recross Pell Run [I] . The
grade now heads SSW and climbs over a saddle [K] . Follow the
grade around the S flank of the hill and head NW. Meet another
trail [M] coming in from the N, and head WNW and then N. Later
head W, with a tributary of Upper Sheriff Run on your right.
At the bottom of the valley is a three-sided lean-to [O] . This
area is referred to as Hunter's Station. Cross a bridge and

continue N along the W side of the run, crossing it shortly
before a nice camping area found in an open area $\boxed{Q}$. Shortly
after the clearing, the trail leaves the RR grade and turns W
to cross Upper Sheriff Run and ascends to FS179 $\boxed{S}$, 0.7mi S of
the gate $\boxed{R}$ at the main highway.
Segment 2: Continue S on FS179 across the saddle. Then, at
the trail sign, enter the woods on your right (SW). Go through
a gate into a fenced area. Here the NCT passes along the side
of a clearcut area. Shortly after leaving the fenced-in area
through another gate $\boxed{T}$, turn W. (FS179 can be seen from this
turn.) The trail then heads SW and descends down the ridge
into Lower Sheriff Run. Pass a few large rocks, including a
nice formation S of the trail. Pass through some open meadows,
then rock-hop across Lower Sheriff Run. A nice campsite is
found here. Climb NW to FS255 $\boxed{U}$.
Segment 3: Cross FS255 and follow the NCT SW \Map 7\ into
Fools Creek Valley through large rock blocks with a memorial
plaque to Ruth Samuelson, past president of Allegheny Outing
Club. Then climb NW over moss-covered rocks just below a large
rock ledge to emerge on Minister Hill Road $\boxed{W}$.

NCT SECT. 7; MINISTER HILL ROAD TO DUNHAM SIDING   5.1mi(8.2km)

SCEN: 2	DIFF: I	COND: A
SKI-: S2	NOTE: B,M,1	ELEV: 1850/1390

MAPS: Cherry Grove, USFS(A), Map 7 in this Guide
TRAIL SEGMENTS:
  (1) Minister Hill Road to Triple Fork Camp   1.5mi
  (2) Triple Fork Camp to FS419   1.8mi
  (3) FS419 to Tanbark Trail   1.8mi

Access: The NCT is signed as it crosses Minister Hill Road
($\boxed{W}$, Map 7), 1.65mi S of Vandergriff Corners and 2 mi N of
Minister on PA666. There is room for a few cars on the road-
side. For the FS419 trail crossing, cars must park at the gate
1.0mi N of the trail (close to the main road). At the FS116
trailhead, parking is possible at a wide spot on the berm large
enough for two cars.
Segment 1: Starting from the E trailhead $\boxed{W}$, proceed SW for
0.1mi, turn W on a straight trail through open woods. Some
blow-down is encountered in this area. Veer SW and pass between a ridge on the right (NW) and a tributary of Minister
Creek on the SE. Note many large and interesting rock formations in this area. Join blue-blazed Minister Valley Trail
from the S $\boxed{X}$. A sign says "Deerlick Camp 1.5mi" E. Follow
blue and white blazes W and then NW to descend diagonally toward the junction of two creeks. Note a large spring along the
trail halfway down the hill. Triple Fork Campground $\boxed{Z}$ is at
the junction of Minister Creek and a tributary. Camping is
possible for large parties. Better camping for small groups is
found further up Minister Creek Valley.

Segment 2: Cross both streams on plank bridges. NCT (white blazes only) bears NW and travels uphill above, and parallel to, the W branch of Minister Creek. Pass large hemlock, maple and black cherry and several springs. The trail, just before [B], now passes through a blow-down from the May 1985 tornado. White vinyl diamonds reroute the trail for a short distance. The trail also passes through a fenced-in blow-down area as shown on Map 7.

Segment 3: Proceed WNW along FS419 for 0.1mi to a point where FS419 turns sharply N. Leave FS419 at a sign post and cross a flat area to the W. Proceed WNW along several easy old logging RR grades. Pass a nice area for primitive camping. Water is common in this area except in very dry periods. After crossing FS116 [D] the NCT turns S, while the Tanbark Trail begins straight ahead.

NCT SECTION 8: DUNHAM SIDING TO KELLETTVILLE   11.6mi(18.7km)

SCEN: 2	DIFF: II	COND: A
SKI-: S4	NOTE: B,M,11	ELEV: 1870/1170

MAPS: Cherry Grove, Cobham, Kellettville, USFA(A), Maps 7, 8
      and 9 in this Guide
TRAIL SEGMENTS:
  (1) Dunham Siding (FS116) to FS449   7.2mi
  (2) FS449 to PA666 (Kellettville)   4.4mi

The lower portion of this section of the NCT has been extensively damaged by horses and ATVs. The Sheffield Ranger District hopes, eventually, to move this lower portion E of Fork Run. (See Map 9.)

Access: The NCT crosses FS116 [D] 0.4mi S of Dunham Siding on the way to Mayburg. The trail sign reads "TANBARK→" and "N.COUNTRY TRAIL ↔". Tanbark Trail starts out at the same spot along FS116. Parking is possible for two cars. FS449 is passable by car. The trail crosses Balltown Road a few miles N of Kellettville, but Balltown Road requires a 4-wheel-drive vehicle. Parking is available for 4-5 cars along PA666 near Kellettville.

Segment 1: Starting from the E trailhead ([E],Map 7), the NCT leaves FS116 and heads S into Queen Creek Valley. Join a logging road and continue downhill on an old RR grade, through a fenced-in blow-down area ([G],Map 8) and follow a side stream SE up to a saddle. Follow an old logging road through flat and open terrain. Descend from the saddle SE down into Coalbed Run Valley. Follow Coalbed Run along its S bank until after the stream turns NW [I]. Then climb S past some windfall.

Turn W and follow along the edge of a large clearcut (dense regrowth). Blazes may be hard to follow here. Turn S and cross the faint remains of an old grassy logging trail. Drop down into the valley leading to Beaver Run, keeping E of the tributary. At the bottom of the valley, near the stream

The North Country Trail between Kellettville and the Baker Trail.   Photo by Carolyn Yattz.

junction ⬚M⬚, cross Beaver Run to its S bank and proceed E
(past a spring?). The stream is scenic and clear, with a sandy
bottom. After 0.5mi climb S up a gentle side valley to FS449
⬚O⬚.

Segment 2: Cross FS449 and go S into East Fork Valley. Join
the old logging road shown on the topo. About 150yd after
joining the road, a large spring ⬚Q⬚ can be reached by turning E
and going 50yd. Follow the old road S past a large clearcut
(dense regrowth) on the W side of the road. At the end of road
⬚S⬚, curve W and climb the hill. Double around the contour and
through a logging landing. Angle up to an OGM road crossing.
Note a shale bank to the right. Re-enter the woods and follow
a snowmobile trail around private property, following orange
diamond blazes \Map 9\. Descend down the next little cove and
angle SW down an old RR grade. Cross the stream near the junction of East and Middle Forks ⬚U⬚.

Stay on the E bank of Fork Run until Balltown Road ⬚V⬚.
Several campsites are found along this stretch. Water in Fork
Run is probably not drinkable because of drilling operations
near Balltown Road. Cross Balltown Road, keeping on the E bank
of Fork Run. Watch for a jog in the trail 50-100yd S of Balltown Road. Continue S along Fork Run. The trail bears E
around and above a beaver dam ⬚W⬚ that has flooded the old
trail route. Creek crossings are frequent, but generally follow the RR grade. At ⬚X⬚, the trail bears up the hillside on
the W side of Fork Run. Climb up to PA666 where there is a
trail sign ⬚Z⬚ 0.8mi N of Tionesta Creek and Kellettville. A
general store is located along PA666 in nearby Whig Hill.

NCT SECTION 9:   KELLETTVILLE TO BAKER TRAIL   18.5mi(29.8km)
SCEN: 1   DIFF: II   COND: B
SKI-: S4   NOTE: B,M,5   ELEV: 1800/1170
MAPS: Kellettville, Mayburg, Marienville West, USFS(A), Maps 9
10 and 11 in this Guide
TRAIL SEGMENTS:
   (1) PA666(Kellettville ⬚Z⬚) to FS127/FS145 ⬚D⬚   2.4mi
   (2) FS127/FS145 to FS145 (game food plots ⬚K⬚)   5.8mi
   (3) FS145 (game food plots) to FS145 (Old NCT ⬚P⬚) 4.1mi
   (4) FS145 (Old NCT) to FS145 (Amsler Spring ⬚T⬚)   2.9mi
   (5) FS145 (Amsler Sp.) to Muzette Road (SR27010) ⬚V⬚ 1.4mi
   (6) Muzette Road to Baker Trail ⬚X⬚   1.7mi
       (Baker Trail ⬚X⬚ to Vowinckle Road (SR27035) ⬚Z⬚ 1.1mi)
or   (Baker Trail ⬚X⬚ to PA66 ⬚Y⬚   2.1mi)

Access: After the road travel on Segment 1, the NCT starts on
FS127 just beyond the junction ⬚D⬚ (Map 9). FS127 is marked as
"The Branch Trail" on the topo. A trail sign is seen here.
Parking is available for two cars. Parking is also available
along FS145 near intermediate access points ⬚K⬚ and ⬚P⬚ (Map
10).

91

At the FS145 junction [T] (Map 11), cars can park in nearby Amsler Springs Picnic Area. The signed trail crossing of Muzette Road [V] is 0.8mi W of the junction of Muzette Road and FS145. Parking is available for two cars at the Muzette Road trail crossing.

Segment 1: At the N trail access ([Z],Map 9) the first 0.8mi of trail uses the berm of PA666 down to Kellettville and Tionesta Creek, following PA666 as it bends NNE and goes upstream at Kellettville. About 0.3mi upstream, a side road [B] crosses Tionesta Creek. Follow the side road to the junction of FS127 and FS145 [D].

Segment 2: From [D], the NCT proceeds E along the grade above FS127 and a stream called "The Branch". The trail soon turns uphill and heads SE. The trail traverses the hillside through extensive damage from the May 1985 tornado. Some good views exist of the tornado damage on the hillsides to the N amd E. Pass through large rock blocks. After reaching the hill top [F] turn S and cross two woods roads in a fairly level area. Continue S, descending gently on an old roadway into a valley of the side stream of Fourmile Run. \Map 10\.

As Fourmile Run is approached, cross the side stream and head E into a clearing on the N bank of Fourmile Run. Proceed through meadows going upstream. After 200yd, cross Fourmile Run [H] and head uphill (ESE). Bear W (right) near the top of the hill. Note an old OGM building on the left as the trail meanders WSW through OGM sites. Just over a gentle rise pass through nice rock blocks and descend through a rocky glen into a side stream valley of Salmon Creek. Traverse several switchbacks [J] going N and S, crossing small tributaries of Salmon Creek. Intersect an old road [K] (This road can be taken SW to FS145.) with adjoining game-food plots.

Segment 3: Follow the road through one remaining switch-back before heading N along an open ridge with good views across Salmon Creek Valley. Then double back (large dog leg) into yet another side stream valley. At the bottom end of this valley reach Guinton Run. Follow Guiton Run upstream, cross [L] and return downstream on the S bank.

Climb and curve S around the hillside, with a view of Salmon Creek Valley. Shortly after the trail crests, turn SSE, then SSW, along and across another tributary--down into Little Salmon Creek Valley [M]. Stay on the N bank, and follow Little Salmon Creek upstream, E. This is a scenic area, with good camping spots. Go upstream for 0.5mi. The trail passes between a stream on the right and a steep hillside on left (N). Cross the stream on a double log bridge [N]. Turn E (left) for a short distance before turning W on an old RR grade. Then angle up the hillside, going over the crest on a switch-back. Intersect the old NCT (now an ATV trail) [P].

Segment 4: Curve S around the hillside above FS145, descending somewhat into another sidestream valley. \Map 11\ Cross a stream at the head of the valley and bend W around the side of

the hill. Turn S through a rocky area and climb to the top of
the large rock overlook (a nice spot for camping or a picnic).
Head SE to a pipeline swath [R]. Continue S past a rock ledge
and descend S into another side stream valley. Head W toward a
meadow. The trail emerges on FS145 [T] in Salmon Creek Valley.
Segment 5: Turn S and follow FS145 150yd to cross Salmon Creek
Bridge. Just S of the bridge the trail goes into the former
Amsler Springs picnic area on the W side of road (1360'). This
is a pleasant area with parking, toilet, lean-to, but no water.
Pass SW through the area and cross an unnamed tributary of
Salmon Creek. The stream parallels FS145. The trail keeps on
the S bank, and soon switch-backs up the hill and levels off,
going past an open area and on to Muzette Road [V] where the
trailhead is signed.
Segment 6: The trail continues across Muzette Road and heads S
on a wood road, then curves SW, crossing a stream through open
grassy, level woods. Near Coon Creek red markers indicate the
Forest boundary and the beginning of State Gamelands No.24.
This is an open area through which Coon Creek flows. The two
ponds on Coon Creek, shown on the topo, no longer exist. Cross
Coon Creek and climb SW up a ridge. Soon you reach a T-junc-
tion [X] with the Baker Trail. This is the S terminus of the
North Country Trail in Allegheny National Forest.
((Segment 7a)): From [X] continue S on the Baker Trail
(condition unknown) to PA66 and to Cook Forest State Park. To
do this, turn left (SE) and, after 100yd, reach a jeep trail
and turn left (ENE) again. Reach PA66 [Y], 1.1mi E of Vowinckel.
((Segment 7b)): A right (NW) turn at the terminus [X] of the
NCT leads 1.1mi NW along a gasline swath to the N terminus [Z]
of the Baker Trail on the Vowinckel-Muzette Road, 3.1mi N of
Vowinckel.

MINISTER CREEK TRAIL   6.5mi(10.5km)
SKI: S4   NOTE: B,M,5   ELEV: 1700/1240
MAPS: Cherry Grove, USFS(A), Map 7 in this Guide
TRAIL SEGMENTS:
  (1) PA666 to Triple Fork Camp (E leg)(NCT)   2.8mi
  (2) Triple Fork Camp (NCT) to PA666 (W leg)   3.7mi

     This loop trail is in the Minister Valley Back Country
Recreation Area. It has a good selection of camp sites in the
upper reaches of the valley and provides opportunity for begin-
ning back-packing. It is one of the more popular trails in the
ANF, especially for backpacking.
Note: The USFS map refers to a "Deerlick Camp" along Minister
Creek at el. 1300, and a trail leading to it from the E. Our
trail scouts, however, noted a blue-blazed side-trail leading
downhill from the E leg of Minister Valley Trail 1.mi further
N--close to NCT.

Rock formation and shelter along Minister Valley Trail. Photo
by John McNavage.

Access: Parking is available for 20-30 cars on the S side of
PA666 across from Minister Creek Campground. The trail begins
in the campground near Minister Creek. FS537 is gated. To
reach the area from Sheffield, drive SE on PA666 for 14.7mi.
The campground at the trailhead is open from April 15 to Decem-
ber 15. There are six sites with fireplaces, picnic tables and
tent pads. Vault toilets and hand-pumped water are available.
The fee is $5.00 (1989). For further information on this camp-
ground see page 37 .

Segment 1: From the PA666 trailhead $\boxed{M}$, proceed N, following
blue blazes along Minister Creek. At 0.9mi cross the creek $\boxed{O}$
on a wood bridge. Climb gradually N and NE, crossing a small
stream $\boxed{P}$ at 1.5mi. The first rock formations of the valley
are found along this part of the trail. The trail follows the
contour of the hillside to another stream crossing $\boxed{R}$ at
2.0mi. Exposed shale in this area contains fossils of shell
fish, as do layers of shale elsewhere along the trail. After
following the contour of the hillside a short distance, the
trail drops into the valley of Minister Creek, meeting North
Country Trail (NCT) at 2.4mi $\boxed{X}$. NCT is blazed with white
paint. Follow the blue and white blazes to a spring at 2.6mi.
The trail descends to Triple Fork Camp, an area of level ground
at the E fork of Minister Creek.

Segment 2: Cross the stream on a single plank at 2.8mi. The
trail turns S, immediately after crossing the W fork on two
planks. The NCT climbs out of the valley at 3.0mi $\boxed{Z}$. Continue following the blue blazes S, along Minister Creek, past
the ruins of an old building. Cross a stream on a rocky section of trail at 3.2mi, and climb gradually to rocky heights.
Rock formations are seen above the trail on the right. Walk
between large rocks and then along the top of the ridge. Minister Valley Overlook is on a large rock on the left side of
the trail at 4.6mi. The trail descends a rock staircase
through spectacular mountain laurel, switches back on the face
of the valley to damp ground at 5.8mi, then proceeds along the
hillside back to Minister Creek and the creek-side trail pro-
ceeding S to the parking lot $\boxed{M}$ at 6.5mi.

TANBARK TRAIL   8.1mi(13.0km)
SCEN: 2   DIFF: II   COND: A
SKI-: S4   NOTE: B,M,2   ELEV: 1890/1060
MAPS: Cherry Grove, Cobham, Youngsville, USFS(A), Maps 7 and
      12 in this Guide
TRAIL SEGMENTS:
  (1) FS116 to Heart's Content Road (FS18)(SR61031?) 0.3mi
  (2) H.C.Road to Heart's Content Road $\boxed{K}$ 2.2mi
  (3) H.C.Road to PA337   2.7mi
  (4) PA337 to Allegheny River (US62)   2.9mi

Tanbark Trail leads W from the NCT, through a portion of the Hickory Creek area, to the Allegheny River and US62. Ironwood Trail has its S terminus near Tanbark Trail's E trailhead. Another side trail lead E into Heart's Content Scenic Area. Just N of the that, Tom Run Loop Trail (now part of Heart's Content Ski-Touring Trail) crosses Tanbark Trail. These two trails follow the same route for 0.3mi near the second crossing of Heart's Content Road. Tanbark Trail is blazed with blue paint blazes. Overall, it is in excellent condition (9/89) and offers pleasant, interesting scenery.

Access: The E end of Tanbark Trail begins at FS116 at a junction with the NCT, near Dunham Siding. To reach this junction, take FS116 S out of Dunham Siding for 0.4mi. A trail sign marks the crossing (D ,Map 7) of the NCT at the edge of clearcut. Parking is available for several cars here. The first (E) junction with Heart's Content Road has no suitable parking. The second (W) junction K with Hearts Content Road has parking space for several cars along the berm. A far better alternative to K is to park cars at the Heart's Content Scenic Area Picnic Area (0.3mi S along FS18). An informal trail shown (ooo) on Map 12 takes off from Hickory Creek Trail in a pine grove (as a blue-blazed ski-touring trail) 50yd S of the picnic area lot, and leads you back to Tanbark Trail. The junction with PA337 has an old picnic area parking lot useful for 6-8 cars. At the W trailhead along US62 parking is possible half-way between Slater and Clark Runs. This W (US62) trailhead is also signed.

Segment 1: Starting from the E, FS116 and the junction D with NCT, Tanbark Trail heads N and crosses Middle Hickory Creek \Map 12\, and climbs up to the hard-surfaced Heart's Content Road (E ,Map 12). Trail signs mark the junction.

Segment (2): After crossing FS18 (SR61031?), Tanbark Trail turns left (WNW), paralleling the road. Ironwood Trail takes off to the N 0.1mi beyond E. (Ironwood Trail is not described in this Guide.) Follow an old woods road and climb the ridge above Heart's Content Road. Drop off the ridge to the N at a saddle. Cross the creek bottom G among hemlock and pine. A flat area, with signs of Heart's Content Scenic Area is visible to the left (W). A side trail leads to the Scenic Area. Shortly after that, the S leg of Tom Run Loop Trail crosses. Climb N over the ridge and drop down to join the N leg of Tom Run Loop Trail I in Tom Run Valley. Turn left (W) with a clearing on the right. After 0.4mi, turn right (NW) off the old RR grade. (A green-diamond-blazed (ski-touring) trail continues straight ahead (SW) at this right turn and leads to Hickory Creek Trail and to the Heart's Content area parking lot/picnic area and to Heart's Content Campground.) Cross a power line swath leading to a pump, and emerge on Hearts Content Road K 0.5mi N of Heart's Content Picnic Area, Scenic Area and Campground. A trail sign marks this trailhead. A short distance SE from the road another sign says: "Minister Valley 6.5mi, Sandstone Springs 2.7mi".

Segment 3: Cross FS18 and enter the woods. A sign says "Sandstone Springs 2.7mi". Proceed NNW up a gentle rise for 0.3mi, then descend among rocks of the valley wall. Laurel covers the hilltops in this part of the Forest. At one point the trail descends into a 20ft-deep, narrow rock crevice and emerges among impressive giant boulders. The trail crosses a pipeline right-of-way and reaches the main branch of East Hickory Creek ⬚M, which is a small, clear, gravel-bottomed stream at this point. Continue N across East Hickory Creek. A good campsite (capacity: 10) is just N of the stream crossing. Nearby, rock walls contain sheltered ledges where people often pitch tents. Climb the ridge. At the top the trail turns S briefly and then turns back N as the topo indicates. Missing blazes (1989) make it tricky to find where the trail direction changes from N to NW here. Use your compass and watch the treadway. Bear NW through laurel at the top of the ridge. Many large rocks overlook the valley here, and the treadway becomes less rocky. The trail leads generally NNW and crosses a small stream ⬚O near an old clearing. Note the 50yd detour (blue-diamond plastic blazes) SW to an easier stream-crossing spot here. Ascend to a shallow saddle on the plateau. Cross a stream on the other side of the saddle. Pass a logging clearing, and drop down to PA337 ⬚P at the abandoned Sandstone Springs picnic ground on the W side of PA337, 0.2mi S from the junction with Heart's Content Road (FS18). About 10yd NE of the PA337 trailhead on the SE side of PA337 is Sandstone Spring under a large hemlock. Motorists often stop to fill jugs here. Across PA337 from Sandstone Spring is the abandoned (but useable) parking lot for the former (yet attractive and useable) Sandstone Springs Picnic Area (no facilities).

Segment 4: Cross PA337 at the trail sign and turn left (W) to join Slater Run Trail (marked on the topo). Still in sight of PA337, turn right (N) onto Slater Run Trail and proceed through open, level, fern-carpeted woods, gradually descending into Slater Run Valley. After 1.0mi, Tanbark Trail leaves Slater Run Trail and turns N across Slater Run ⬚R, continuing over the hill to the upper reaches of Boarding House Run where it joins a continuation of a trail (marked on the topo) coming in from the radio towers to the (SE) on PA337. The trail runs (NW) on the S side of Boarding House Run down to the Allegheny River and US62. Pass a large clearing on the opposite side of the stream. The trail then descends through attractive hemlock forest, past scenic conglomerate rock formations and cascades. On the final descent to the Allegheny River the woods road bends away to the left while the trail drops straight down along Boarding House Run. Resistant rock above the Allegheny gives rise to more interesting formations and cascades. The end of the trail ⬚T is signed at US62.

TOM RUN LOOP TRAIL   3.6mi(5.8km)
SCEN: 2   DIFF: I   COND: A
SKI-: S2   NOTE: B,M,0   ELEV:1910/1620
MAPS: Cherry Grove, USFS(A), Maps 7 and 12 in this Guide
TRAIL SEGMENTS:
  (1) Hearts Content Picnic Area to Ironwood Trail [F]   1.2mi
  (2) Ironwood Trail to Tanbark Trail [I]   1.5mi
  (3) Tanbark Trail to H.C. Picnic Area   0.9mi

       This pleasant route along old logging roads should be kept
in mind when planning hikes along the Tanbark Trail or loop
hikes from the Heart's Content area or the Hickory Creek area.
The Forest Service has renamed Tom Run Trail. It is now a portion of the "Hearts Content Ski-Touring Trail" which is about
twice as long. (The new, longer route is not described in this
Guide. The Forest Service should have maps soon.)
Access: Park cars at the Hearts Content Picnic Area parking
lot on Heart's Content Road (FS18) across from Hearts Content
Campground.
Segment 1: Starting from the picnic area, follow the blue tri-
angles W into the woods past the out-houses and close to the N
boundary of Hearts Content Scenic Area. After 0.4mi cross Tanbark Trail [H](Map 12) and soon come to the RR grade along the
head of the W Branch of Tionesta Creek through a tunnel of hemlocks. Pass the N terminus of Ironwood Trail [F](Map 7).
Segment 2: Bear NW following a small stream to the junction
with Tom Run [J]. Here one could take a side trail (See
description on page 112) ENE and N to Chapman Dam State Park
along the W Branch of Tionesta Creek through State Gamelands
29. Instead, bear NW, up Tom Run. Soon join Tanbark Trail [I]
(Map 12) for 0.3mi to where Tanbark Trail departs to the NW to
cross Hearts Content Road [K].
Segment 3: Follow an old logging grade SE to join Hickory
Creek Trail for 0.1mi through a red pine plantation back to the
Picnic Area.

HEARTS CONTENT SCENIC AREA TRAIL   1.0mi(1.6km)
SCEN: 1   DIFF: I   COND: A
SKI-: S2   NOTE: I   ELEV: 1900/1800
MAPS: Cobham, USFS(A), Map 12 in this Guide
SEGMENTS: (loop starting at the picnic area parking lot)

       Heart's Content Scenic Area began as a 20-acre donation of
virgin timber from the lumber company of Wheeler and Dusenbury
in 1929. An additional 101 acres was purchased in 1931. The
area was designated as a National Natural Landmark in July,
1977. The adjacent picnic area, a 158-acre tract, known as
Wilken's Farm, was donated to the Forest Service in 1934 by the
State Federation of Pennsylvania Women.

Scene along the loop trail in the Heart's Content Scenic Area.
Photo by John McNavage.

An interpretive trail leads through this beautiful 121-acre (0.2 sq.mi) tract of virgin timber. Some hemlocks here are over 350 years old, and nearly 4 feet across. There are also huge white pines. The area has never been timbered and is well-worth a visit from both an aesthetic and an educational perspective.

Access: The trail begins in the picnic area just off Heart's Content Road (FS18) (gravel) and across FS18 from Heart's Content Campground, 4.mi E of PA337.

Segment 1: The trail route is not described here since the treadway is always obvious due to the heavy use. Be sure to remain on the trail here because the area receives extremely heavy use in late spring through October.

HICKORY CREEK AREA

The Hickory Creek Area encompasses most of the upper watershed of East Hickory Creek, a moderate-sized stream emptying into the Allegheny River, and its principal tributary, Middle Hickory Creek. It is due E of Tidioute in the Sheffield Ranger District. The terrain is gentle. Gravel and narrow paved roads encircle the 20 sq.mi roadless area, roughly following the drainage divides of East and Middle Hickory Creeks. In-holdings comprise only about 1 sq.mi. of the total and, with one exception, all are on the perimeter along the roads.

In October of 1984, 13.4 of the 20sq.mi of Hickory Creek roadless area were declared by Congress to be a Wilderness area with the passage of the Pennsylvania Wilderness Act. As a result, no motorized or mechanized uses of any kind are permitted. Horseback riding is not permitted on Hickory Creek Trail but is permitted elsewhere. The primary attraction of the Wilderness is Middle Hickory Creek with its bogs and beaver ponds, and with large white pine scattered in open areas. As the trees grow bigger, the Wilderness will grow in its natural appeal.

Hickory Creek Wilderness was hit by a tornado on May 31, 1985. This blew down 1.1sq.mi of forest along the S boundary of the Wilderness. The blow-down was left there to provide a graphic illustration of the power wielded by a tornado.

The main access to the Wilderness is Heart's Content Campground along FS18. One can also gain access at the W end from FS119. (See Big Side Loop Trail.) Hunting, fishing and camping are permitted in the Wilderness. The streams contain natural populations of brown trout and brook trout.

Much of the area is heavily forested with beech, hemlock, oaks, hickory, and other hardwoods. Giant chestnut snags stand at higher elevations. Groves of hemlock, some quite large, grow along the lower parts of East Hickory Creek and its downstream tributaries, and scattered white pine are found in open areas along both streams. The banks of East Hickory Creek are mostly forested, but there are several bogs and meadows (savannahs) along its upper end. Middle Hickory, in contrast,

flows through a meadow studded with bogs and beaver ponds for
most of its length. Jack's Run, one of the principal side
streams, is bordered by a chain of attractive small meadows.

Besides beaver, the area supports black bear and one of
the largest turkey populations in the Forest. Deer are numerous. East Hickory Creek has been designated a Wilderness Trout
Stream by the Pennsylvania Fish Commission. The Commission
hopes that in order to preserve native brook trout these
streams will not be stocked; they will be left undisturbed for
fishermen who prefer to "rough it" in wilderness surroundings.

Logging in the area began more than 100 years ago, and
there may have been scattered small farms as late as the
1930's, when the federal government acquired the surface
rights. Some mineral rights remain in private hands, although
the mineral rights under Hickory Creek Wilderness were purchased by the government several years after 1984 when Wilderness status was achieved.

The Hickory Creek (loop) Trail is described below. It is
a formal (USFS-maintained) trail that is marked on Maps 8 and
12 with solid circles (●) to the W and S of Hearts Content
Campground. Unfortunately this trail does not lead the hiker
along two of the most popular and scenic attractions of the
area--Middle Hickory Creek and East Hickory Creek. These two
streams can be reached in several ways from Hickory Creek
Trail. These are also described below, along with descriptions
of the stream-side trails themselves. These informal (not
USFS-maintained) trails are shown on Maps 8 and 12 with open
circles (o).

HICKORY CREEK TRAIL   11.5mi(18.5km)
SCEN: 1   DIFF: I-II   COND: B
SKI-: S2   NOTE: B,M   ELEV: 1950/1450
MAPS: Cobham, USFS(A), Maps 8 and 12 in this Guide
TRAIL SEGMENTS:
  (1) Picnic Area to Big Side Loop Trail [U]   1.8mi
  (2) [U] to Little Side Loop Trail (Coon Run)   2.5mi
  (3) Coon Run to Jack's Run [D]   2.1mi
  (4) [D] to Big Side Loop Trail [Z]   4.0mi
  (5) [Z] to Heart's Content Picnic Area   1.1mi

The USFS opened this loop trail on July 1, 1978. The N
half of this loop runs along the plateau between the valleys of
East Hickory Creek and Middle Hickory Creek. This portion
could be used for ski-touring since it is reasonably level.
The S half of the trail climbs in and out of several small
stream valleys that drain into Middle Hickory Creek. The woods
are fairly open in many areas here. There are also some clearings for camping, but many people prefer to camp in the open
areas closer to Middle Hickory Creek.

An interesting side trip (alternate route) involves using

Jacks Run, Coon Run (open woods) and the old RR grade along
Middle Hickory Creek. Along this creek are broad, open meadows, bogs, beaver ponds, giant Hemlocks, etc. (See Hickory
Creek Area.) Some remains of the old logging days early in
this century are to be seen at various points along Hickory
Creek Trail (e.g. locomotive wheels). A blow-down (1979) on
the E leg of the trail 0.5mi N of the southern-most point may
cause a minor detour. Jacks Run and Coon Run areas are
reported to be the most interesting parts of the trail. The
trail is in the Sheffield Ranger District (814-968-3232).
Access: The best access to Hickory Creek Trail is the Heart's
Content Picnic Area/Scenic Area which is on the opposite side
of Heart's Content Road from Heart's Content Campground. The
trail crosses Heart's Content Road a short distance N of the
turnoff to the picnic area and 300yd S of where Tanbark Trail
(blue-blazed) crosses Heart's Content Road. Hickory Creek
Trail is blazed in yellow. Those hiking along Middle Hickory
Creek will find easy walking, through open woods, up Jacks Run
or Coon Run to gain access to Hickory Creek Trail from the S
(FS119).
Segment 1: The entire trail is easy to follow, so no need is
seen to describe the route here.

LITTLE SIDE LOOP OF HICKORY CREEK TRAIL   3.9mi(6.3km)
SKI: S2   NOTE: B,M,2   ELEV: 1700/1330
MAPS: Cobham, USFS(A), Maps 8 and 12 in this Guide
TRAIL SEGMENTS:
 (1) Hickory Creek Trail to East Hickory Creek (E leg)   2.4mi
 (2) East Hickory Creek to Hickory Creek Trail (W leg)   1.5mi

Access: There is no car access to this trail. Park cars at
the Heart's Content Scenic Area Picnic Area and follow Hickory
Creek Trail to its S leg from which Little Side Loop departs.
Access from the W (FS119) is possible. See the Big Side Loop
trail description below.
Segment 1: At the point where Hickory Creek Trail crosses Coon
Run, turn S along Coon Run. After 50yd find an old abandoned
RR grade. Follow this down Coon Run to Middle Hickory Creek.
Coon Run Valley has plenty of good camp sites.
    Along Middle Hickory Creek runs another old RR grade.
Since this grade intermittently crosses Middle Hickory Creek,
you may prefer to stick to the N side of the creek as it meanders through the park-like valley with open meadows interspersed with hemlocks. Follow this old RR grade W. At the unnamed side-stream coming down from the N, 1.0mi W of Coon Run,
is a beaver pond (A ,Map 8). A wet area is encountered
shortly before the junction with East Hickory Creek B , but at
this point a logging trail climbs the hillside to skirt the
problem and then drops again into the broad right-of-way which
leads to the fork of East- and Middle Hickory Creeks.

102

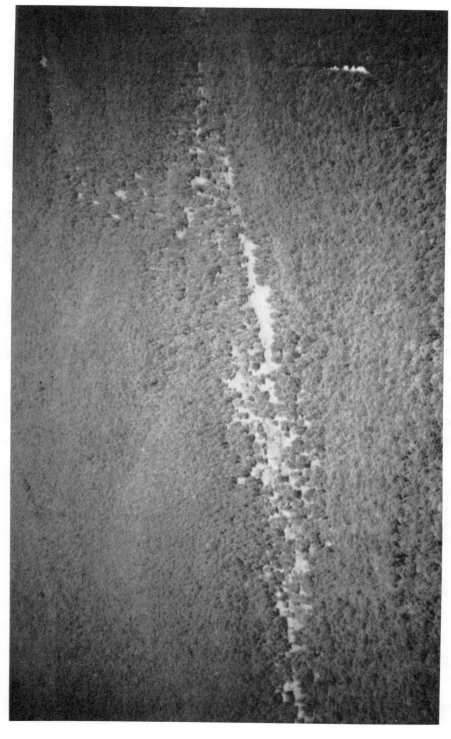

Hickory Creek Area Aerial View. Photo courtesy of the U.S.Forest Service

Segment 2: The RR grade up East Hickory Creek branches off to
the N shortly before the above-mentioned fork. About 0.5mi N
along East Hickory Creek RR grade is another fork [C] where the
grade divides to either side of an enormous hemlock. Take the
right branch, which leads up Jacks Run. This grade is easily
followed up Jacks Run to Hickory Creek Trail ([D],Map 12).

BIG SIDE LOOP OF HICKORY CREEK TRAIL   11.2mi(18.0km)
SKI-: S4   NOTE: B,M,13   ELEV: 1840/1320
MAPS: Cobham, USFS(A), Maps 8 and 12 in this Guide
TRAIL SEGMENTS:
     (Picnic Area to Big Side Loop Trail [U]   1.8mi)
 (1) Hickory Creek Trail [U] to Little Side Loop   2.6mi
 (2) Little Side Loop to East Hickory Creek   1.8mi
 (3) East Hickory Creek to Hickory Creek Trail [Z] 6.8mi
     (Hickory Creek Trail [Z] to H.C. Picnic Area 1.1mi)

     The total loop, starting from Hearts Content Campground,
would cover 14.1mi. This is best regarded as a leisurely two-
day backpack trip.
Access: Same as Little Side Loop
Segment 1: Follow Hickory Creek Trail S from Hearts Content
Campground (Map 12) for 1.0mi and cross a small stream. Proceed 0.2mi further and leave Hickory Creek Trail [U], heading S
to an unnamed stream valley. Walking along this stream for a
short distance leads to an old RR grade leading to Middle Hickory Creek. \Map 8\ Take this grade S, then turn W and follow
the grade along Middle Hickory Creek to Coon Run where Little
Side Loop comes in from the N.
Segment 2: Continue W along Middle Hickory Creek. Because
Middle Hickory Creek is difficult to cross at times, stay on
the N side instead of following the old RR grade back and forth
across Middle Hickory Creek. At the unnamed side stream coming
down from the N 1.0mi W of Coon Run is a beaver pond ([A],Map
8). A wet area is encountered shortly before the junction with
East Hickory Creek [B].
Segment 3: At the junction [B] of East Hickory Creek and Mid-
dle Hickory Creek, cross East Hickory Creek to its W bank.
(From here you could take the old RR grade SW along Hickory
Creek 1.8mi to FS119 near a picnic area.) Along lower Middle
Hickory Creek are pools suitable for swimming.
     From [B] proceed N along the W bank of East Hickory Creek.
There is no trail, but it's easy going with only sparse under-
growth. After 0.8mi an old RR grade comes across to your (W)
side of East Hickory Creek. Follow this RR grade (somewhat
overgrown in places) which is readily passable. Some small
meadows appear along this portion of the route.
     At a stream crossing ([V],Map 12) (1.2mi along the RR
grade that rejoined you) is a small bridge. Continue from here
along the SE side East Hickory Creek. For the next 1.5mi the

trail crosses open meadows punctuated by small dense groves of hemlock. At an old logging camp (indicated on Map 12) don't cross the creek; stay on the SE side. The old RR grade crosses and recrosses in this area. After rejoining the old RR grade, proceed 0.4mi further and cross East Hickory Creek ⬚W to the N bank. Cross a pipeline and soon note a beaver pond.

Shortly after the beaver pond, take an old RR spur ⬚X that turns S, away from East Hickory Creek, and up an unnamed tributary. After a small waterfall, cross to the E bank of this stream. After 0.5mi the trail heads uphill, away from the stream. After a short distance it turns abruptly right and soon meets another trail ⬚Y. Turn SE onto this trail. After 0.5mi rejoin Hickory Creek Trail ⬚Z that you left 11.mi back.

OLD NORTH COUNTRY TRAIL   30.mi(48.km)
MAPS: Marienville West, Mayburg, Lynch, Russell City, USFS(A),
      Maps 10, 14 and 15 of this Guide

      Old NCT is no longer maintained as a hiking trail by the Forest Service. It has been converted into an ATV trail. It is deleted here at the recommendation of the Forest Service.

ALLEGHENY FRONT NATIONAL RECREATION AREA
SKI: S4   NOTE: B,M   ELEV: 1900/1080
MAPS: Cobham, Warren, Youngville, USFS(A), Map 12 in this Guide
      The Allegheny Front Area affords some of the best opportunities for off-trail hiking on the ANF. It is one of the three largest areas (including Hickory Creek Wilderness and the Tracy Ridge area) in the Forest which are substantially roadless, without major utility right-of-ways and OGM sites. The Allegheny Front is the least known but the most interesting of the three. Its features include numerous massive and striking rock formations, beautiful stream valleys small and large, placid waters and steep cascades, woodland openings, and steep slopes which descend to the Allegheny River. It is accorded partial protection as a National Recreation Area.
      Long rock ledges are found S of Slater Run and above the Allegheny River S of Clark Run. Slater Run and Hedgehog Run have large and attractive stream valleys. Charley Run, Boarding House Run and Clark Run are quite open. A large meadow, the site of a former sawmill, is at the junction of Slater and South Slater Run (⬚S,Map 12). A large open area is on high ground near the Tanbark Trail where it crosses the upper reaches of Boarding House Run. There are large trees below the rock ledges (noted on Map 12) above Slater Run.
      The only developed trail is the W segment of the Tanbark Trail, which extends from the former Sandstone Spring Picnic Area on PA337 to the Allegheny River and US62. An old trail up Slater Run can be followed all the way from US62 to PA337 below

Allegheny Front Area from the Allegheny River.   Photo by Sam Hays

Sandstone Spring. Another old trail along South Slater Run leads onto private land.

A trail up Clark Run is another good route from US62, emerging behind houses on PA337, but access to FS573 is possible. A jeep road up Charley Run from US62 does not go through. An old pipeline between US62 and Lenhart Run can be walked.

One pleasant loop hike (Map 12) follows the Tanbark Trail from Sandstone Spring almost to US62, including the descent through conglomerate rock formations. Where Tanbark Trail turns right off the Boarding House Run logging grade to drop to US62, stay left on the grade, wrapping around the hillside and starting back up above Slater Run. This route stays up above Slater Run and does not descend into the meadow [S] at South Slater Run. The route climbs steadily through scenic woods. After passing an old OGM site, it crosses to the right bank of Slater Run and soon meets the Tanbark Trail. ([R],Map 12)

A particularly interesting route follows Tanbark Trail from Sandstone Spring, continuing straight on the Slater Trail until it, too, crosses Slater Run [R]. Then climb WSW to the E end of the rock ledge area marked on Map 12 short of the hilltop. Walk along the base of the ledges, admiring the huge rock formations, big trees and rhododendron. Eventually you descend along the ridge line to its end at the junction [S] of South Slater and Slater Run. (One can also cut further E to explore the valley of South Slater Run.) Cross the meadow [S], and climb steeply up the opposite slope to the logging grade described above which returns you to [R].

With a car shuttle, one can go N from Boarding House Run's upper reaches to the ridge and follow it through more rocks down to the river. Return via Clark Run to FS573. This point can also be reached starting from Hedgehog Trail at US62. One can also reach Hedgehog Run by hiking up Charley Run and cutting S over the wooded ridge from the headwaters. This part of Hedgehog Run is attractive.

BEAVER MEADOWS HIKING TRAIL SYSTEM   6.8mi(10.9km)
SCEN: 1-2   DIFF: I   COND: A
SKI-: S1-S2   NOTE: M,0   ELEV: 1770/1670
MAPS: Lynch, USFS(A), Map 24 in this Guide
TRAIL SEGMENTS (Interconnections not indicated):
 (1) Salmon Creek Loop   [A]   1.3mi
 (2) Seldom Seen Trail   [B]   1.1mi
 (3) Penoke Path   [C]   1.0mi
 (4) Beaver Meadows Loop   [D]   3.0mi
 (5) Lakeshore Loop   [E]   0.4mi

The Beaver Meadows Hiking Trail System consists of five separate, but interconnected, foot trails which center around the area's focal point--Beaver Meadows Lake (37 acres). A campground is located on the N side of the lake. It is an

ideal spot to spend a quiet weekend, and the trails are within
easy walking distance of the campsites. Deer, beavers, porcu-
pines, wild turkey, Canada geese and great blue herons are common in the area. The hiking trails were constructed by the
Youth Conservation Corps during the summers of 1985-1989. Most
of the forest cover in the area is maple, hemlock and black
cherry. A savannah adds interest to the area. (See page 6 .)
An informal trail (not USFS-maintained) runs through the area
from PA66 to Seldom Seen Corners.

Access: Drive 4.mi N from Marienville on FS128. Turn E on
FS282. Drive 1.0mi to Beaver Meadows Lake and the campground.

Segment 1: Salmon Creek Loop [A] (blue-blazed) begins at the
far end of the dam. Head S, straight uphill fron the foot-
bridge. Pass through a stand of red pine that was planted in
the 1930s by the Civilian Conservation Corps. Following that
is a smaller stand of white spruce.

Segment 2: Seldom Seen Trail [B] (blue-blazed) begins and ends
on Beaver Meadows Loop Trail. It has a planting of blueberries
at [G] for the feeding of bear, deer and hikers.

Segment 3: Penoke Path [C] (blue-blazed) is surrounded by a
large savannah, offering excellent bird-watching opportunities.
Both ends of the trail are on the Beaver Meadows Loop Trail.

Segment 4: Beaver Meadows Loop [D] (grey-blazed) goes com-
pletely around the lake and intersects all other trails. It
crosses Penoke Run on a floating boardwalk that takes you
across a savannah. Blueberries are found, in season, on the S
side of the boardwalk [F].

Segment 5: Lakeshore Loop [E] (blue-blazed) is on the S shore
of Beaver Meadows Lake and starts on Beaver Meadows Loop Trail.

PA66 to Seldom Seen Corners   5.5mi(8.8km)

All but the first mile of this trail is shown on Map 24 as
open circles (o o o o). It is an informal (not USFS-maintained) trail and is not blazed, so it is more appropriate for
more experienced hikers. The trail follows a nice route
through the remote valley of Penoke Run with wide-open vistas
and a variety of forest types. Begin on PA66 1.1mi SW of the
Marienville Fire Tower or 2.1mi NE of Marienville at FS106.
Parking is available on the broad shoulder.

Follow gated FS106 1.0mi N to a water impoundment ([I] on
the S edge of Map 24). The last 0.2mi coincides with a snowmobile trail. Keep to the left side of the clearing below the
dam for 80yd. There, watch for a small fill and openings into
the woods. Do not cross the outlet of the pond. Go in a few
steps and turn left (N) onto an old RR grade.

The grade is clear for another 1.0mi through black cherry-
red maple woods and a planting of large spruce. Ignore orange
and yellow tags on trees. About 1.0mi from the pond the trail
shows some old vehicle use and turns sharp left, but the RR
grade you want to follow goes straight ahead. It is obscure

here because spruce have been planted on the RR grade. (If you miss this point you'll find yourself going uphill into a hard-woods stand. Go back.) The RR grade (correct path) becomes obvious again beyond the spruces and passes through a large opening. As it enters the spruces again, the blue-blazed Penoke Loop Trail joins it from the left [C], and both trails go on to a unique floating bridge over the marsh at the head of Beaver Lake.

The grey-blazed Beaver Meadows Trail meets the RR grade at the bridge. Since the RR grade is flooded by the lake here and along the N shore, follow Beaver Meadows Trail as it winds through a spruce plantation and along some hardwoods, then crosses a stream on a bridge, and goes through red pines until it comes to the RR grade again [K]. Beaver Meadows Trail turns left (S) on the grade, but turn right to follow the trail N. (To shorten the hike, the marked Beaver Meadows Trail could be taken S to Beaver Meadows Picnic Area on either the S side or the N side of the lake.) The grade N goes through a large opening and meets a little-used road which is followed out to Seldom Seen Corners. The trail ends at the Job Corps Road [M] N of Marienville, directly opposite FS127.

OTHER POINTS OF INTEREST FOR HIKERS IN SOUTHWESTERN ALLEGHENY NATIONAL FOREST

Bluejay Creek

The paved road from Pigeon (on PA66 6mi NE from Marien-ville) goes right along Bluejay Creek and some pleasant scenery. At the bridge over Bluejay Creek 3.0mi N of Pigeon one can park and walk upstream along an old logging grade on the NE bank of Bluejay Creek (E side of road) for at least 0.5mi and probably much farther.

About a mile further N along the paved road is another bridge over Bluejay Creek where one can park and enjoy rapids and waterfalls.

Tionesta Fish Hatchery

This State fish hatchery is located along US62 1.0mi N of Tionesta. It is open to visitors. There are indoor displays and huge concrete tanks filled with a wide variety of fish that will be used for stocking streams in NW Pennsylvania.

Tionesta Creek Swimming Hole

A USFS day-use area (no camping, no fires) is found along the NW bank of Tionesta Creek 4.mi SW of Kellettville (at the spot on the map where the gravel road turns sharply from an E-W direction to a N-S direction). A pleasant swimming hole is found here (clear, running water, gravel bottom). It is popular with the natives. The USFS apparently doesn't make its existence known on any of its maps and literature, possibly to prevent over-use, or because of the lack of a life guard. Another more informal swimming area is about 1.mi upstream (NE), just downstream of an old bridge pier visible from the road.

On the NW side of the road, across from the USFS day-use area, is a foot (horse) trail leading NNW along the WSW side of a small tributary of Tionesta Creek. This trail is reputed to go to a horse livery on PA666 just SE of Whig Hill. The trail setting is a scenic stream valley full of large hemlocks.

Tornado Damage Overlook

About 2.5mi SW of Whig Hill on paved SR27007 leading to Tionesta is an overlook that the Forest Service developed to show the devastation of a 5/31/85 tornado. The tornado swath extends E toward Kellettville.

Anders Run Natural Area Walk

Anders Run is a few miles S of Buckaloons Campground on the W side of the Allegheny River. This 96-acre tract of land was acquired in 1987 by the W. Pa. Conservancy. A 0.4mi walking trail goes up the run. The main attractions are the old-growth (170 years old) white pine and hemlock. Some trees are 120 feet high and have trunks over three feet in diameter.

To get to the area, drive N from Tionesta on US62 for about 30mi. Turn left onto a narrower road immediately after US62 crosses the Allegheny River. Proceed past the Allegheny National Forest Research Station (on the left), and National Forge Company (on the right). At the first intersection past National Forge, turn left onto Dunn's Eddy River Road, and follow it for just over a mile to a "Y" intersection with a dirt road called Allegheny Spring Road. Bear right onto the dirt road and proceed 0.2mi to a wooden sign on the left identifying Ander's Run Natural Area. Park here, being careful not to block the dirt road. The area is on the Youngsville topo.

A more complete description of the area is available for $1.00 from the W. Pa. Conservancy, 316 Fourth Avenue, Pittsburgh, PA 15222. Ask for a list of outing guides they sell.

Tidioute Overlook

A mile or two out of Tidiouts on PA337 is an outstanding USFS overlook of the Allegheny River Valley. Near the overlook are picnic tables and pit toilets.

Typical scene in the open bogs and meadows of the Hickory Creek
Area. Photo courtesy of the U.S.Forest Service.

Buckaloons Recreation Area

This recreation area is on the site of a former indian village, on the W bank of the Allegheny River. To reach it, take US6 W from Warren for six miles to PA62. A 1.0mi foot trail, the Seneca Interpretive Trail, circles the recreation area. The area is in the Sheffield Ranger District. (Address and telephone number on page 25) For information on camping facilities see page 37 .

Chapman Dam State Park
MAPS: USFS(A), Warren, Cherry Grove, Map 25 in this Guide

This state park is within the proclamation boundary of Allegheny National Forest so it is appropriate to make note of it in this Guide. It is a few miles S of Warren off US6. It is surrounded by State Gamelands #29 or National Forest lands. Six foot-trails are found in this park. Below is a brief description of each.

Hunters Ridge   (2.8mi, orange blazes) [H]
Half of this trail is rugged and hilly. It has interesting geological features, including fossils.

Adams Run Trail (2.9mi, yellow blazes) [J]
Half of this trail is rugged and hilly.

Lowlands Trail   (0.2mi, blue-on-white blazes) [L]
This is an easy trail across a foot bridge over the W Branch of Tionesta Creek, in and through a wetlands area above the lake.

Lumber Trail   (0.4mi, red blazes) [N]
This trail is a portion of the snowmobile trail which runs from Kinzua Dam to Marienville. It is not a loop trail.

Nature Trail   (1.7mi, white blazes)
Loop 1 (0.7mi) [P] has only a few grades, but Loop 2 [Q] has stairs steps and steep grades. Loop 1 is a self-guided inter-pretive trail with a brochure (describing the designated points of interest) available from the park office. Group guided tours can be arranged in advance by contacting the park office (814-723-5030).

Gamelands Trail (2.3mi, green-on-white blazes)
This trail is level. It runs from the public boat-mooring area, up the State Gamelands service road along the N side of the W Branch of Tionesta Creek into State Gamelands 29. Then it crosses to the S side of the creek [S] and meets and follows an old RR grade into the campground. Return to the starting point by crossing the Lowlands Trail (2.3mi), or make a com-plete circle around Chapman Lake (4.0mi) by using Park Service roads, the breast of the dam, and the public road to the boat-launching/mooring area.

Hearts Content-Chapman State Park Trail   7.0mi(11.3km)
MAPS: USFS(A), Cherry Grove, Maps 7, 12 and 25 in this Guide

This informal (not USFS-maintained) trail connects the trail system in Chapman State Park (See above) to the popular trail system around Heart's Content Scenic Area (Tanbark Trail, Tom Run Trail, Ironwood Trail, Hickory Creek Trail). It is shown as open circles on Maps 7, 12 and 25 (Note a small gap between Maps 12 and 25.) Most of the trail is on State Game-lands #29. The trail is not blazed and is largely cross-coun-try through open woods (black cherry). So avoid this trail in late summer before the first frost because of the tall grass, ferns and wild flowers. The woods have lots of serviceberry that is usually in beautiful full bloom during the first week in May.

Leave a car near the gate at the parking lot on the NW side of Chapman Dam. Start walking from the Heart's Content Picnic Area, using Tom Run Trail to get to $\boxed{J}$, the junction of Tom Run and West Branch of Tionesta Creek. Here turn downhill (NE) toward Davis Run. Get on the N bank of West Branch of Tionesta Creek. From here the route goes along the foot of the hill or in the flat next to the creek. If you prefer, you could cross the Creek to get on FS536 (closed to vehicles by gates at both ends) along the creek. This road would be excel-lent for ski-touring.

The valley becomes marshy near Jones Run, so stay off the flat there. Traces of an old RR grade may be followed part of the way between Jones Run and Conklin Run. This area is par-ticularly nice when serviceberry is blooming. Soon after Con-klin run, cross a gated road $\boxed{A}$ coming down from PA337. The Game Commission has a fenced nursery and a game food plot on the far side of the creek. Pass them and continue across Shaw Run. The woods are denser here with more hemlock, but there are still wet spots in places.

As you approach Wildcat Run you encounter a sulphur spring at the base of the hill, one of three in Warren County. Con-tinuing, you will come to a logging road. (If you come to Wildcat Run first, follow it upstream to the logging road. Turn right on this road and cross Wildcat Run on a bridge. At the intersection $\boxed{C}$ immediately after, take the second right and follow it to the end. (The first road is FS536 which comes all the way down the West Branch of Tionesta Creek.)

Snowmobile-Hiking Trail Loop--The NCT Near Henrys Mills

Some snowmobile routes make acceptable foot trails in the spring and fall. They tend to be too hot in the summer since they usually aren't tree-shaded. The trail described below is shown on Map 6.

Follow the NCT from Henrys Mills NW to the crossing of Pell Run $\boxed{I}$. Continue N along Pell Run a short distance to a pipeline. Turn right (E) onto the pipeline corridor. Cross OGM roads and Duck Eddy Run. Then turn right (SE) on another pipeline and drop down to an old RR grade above Tionesta Creek. Follow this grade S back to the NCT trailhead at Henrys Mills.

Snowmobile-Hiking Trail Loop--The NCT Near FS262

This loop route is shown on Maps 3 and 4. Follow the NCT S from FS262 to Gibbs Hill crossing [C] (Map 3). Continue on the NCT until you reach a snowmobile trail intersecting from the left (open circles on Map 4). Turn NE onto the snowmobile trail and FS261 and proceed downhill, crossing PA321. Then follow an old RR grade with orange diamond snowmobile blazes N, then NNW until you cross PA321 again at FS262, near where the NCT crosses FS262.

Great Stone Face guards two young hikers along Tanbark Trail, northwest of Heart's Content Scenic Area.

The North Country Trail a few miles north of Kellettville. Photo by Bruce Sundquist.

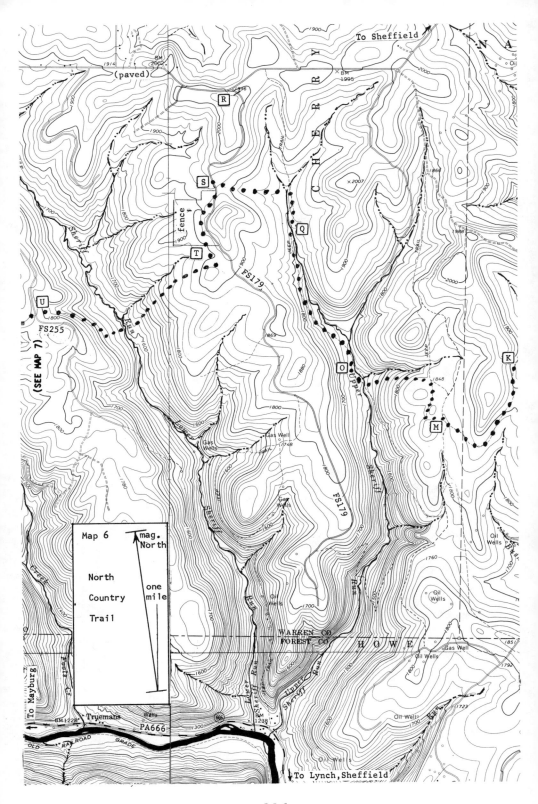

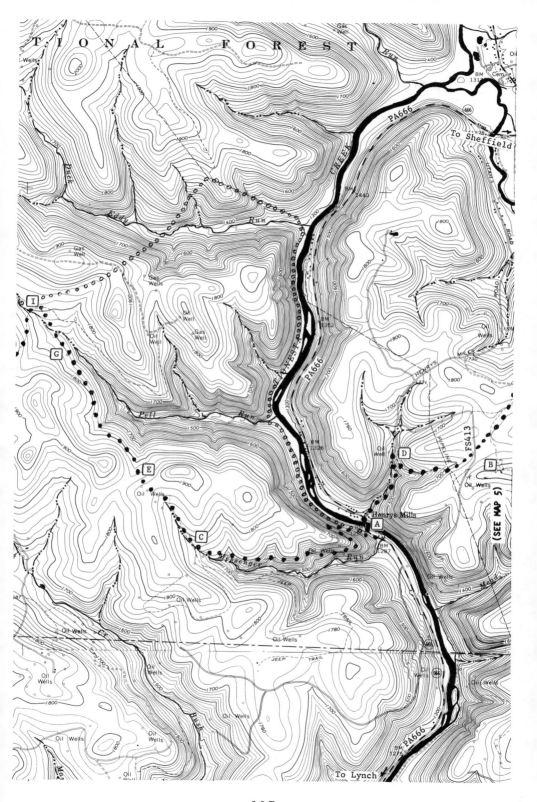

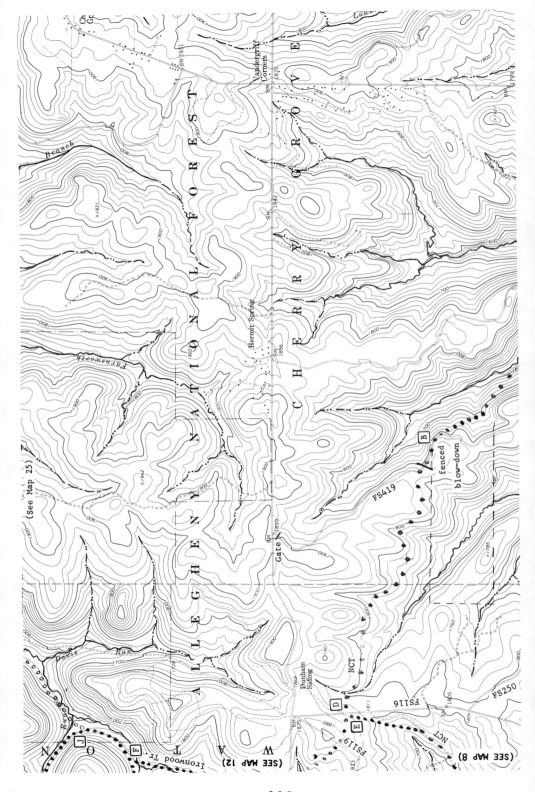

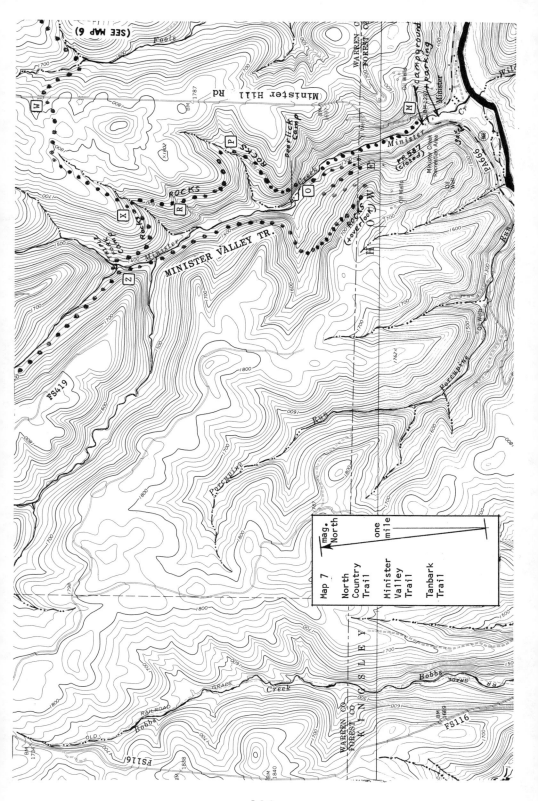

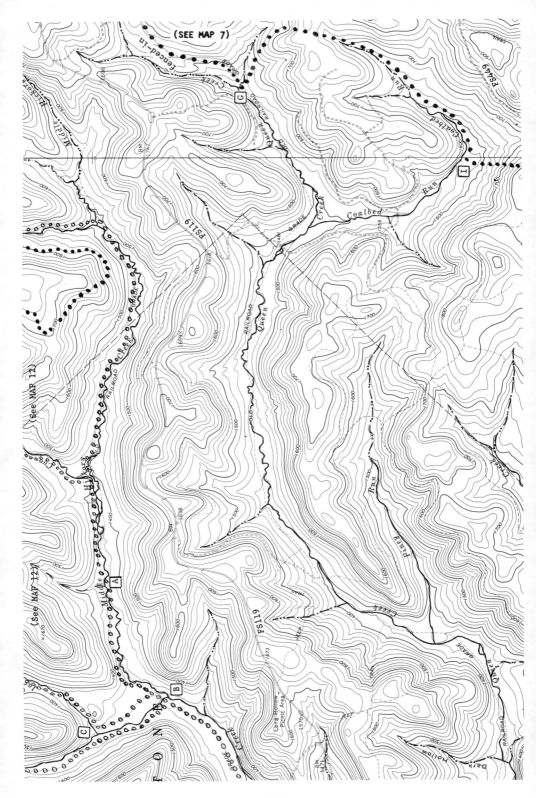

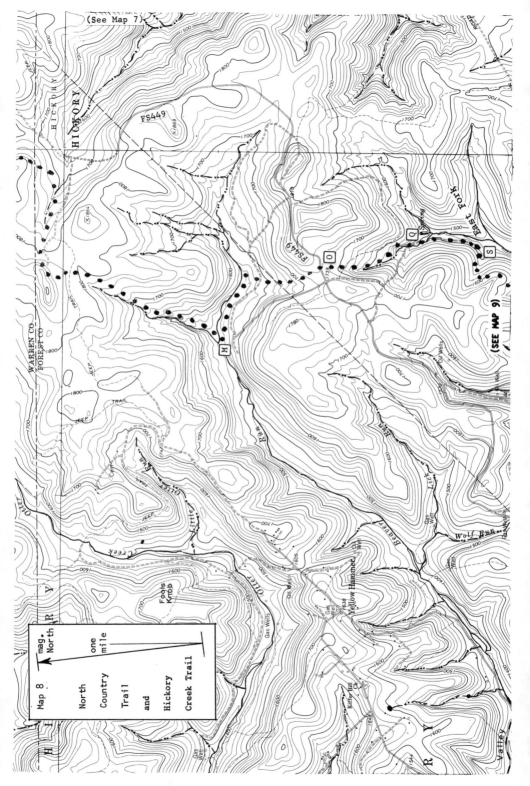

Map 8.

North

Country

Trail

and

Hickory

Creek Trail

mag.
North

one
mile

(SEE MAP 9)

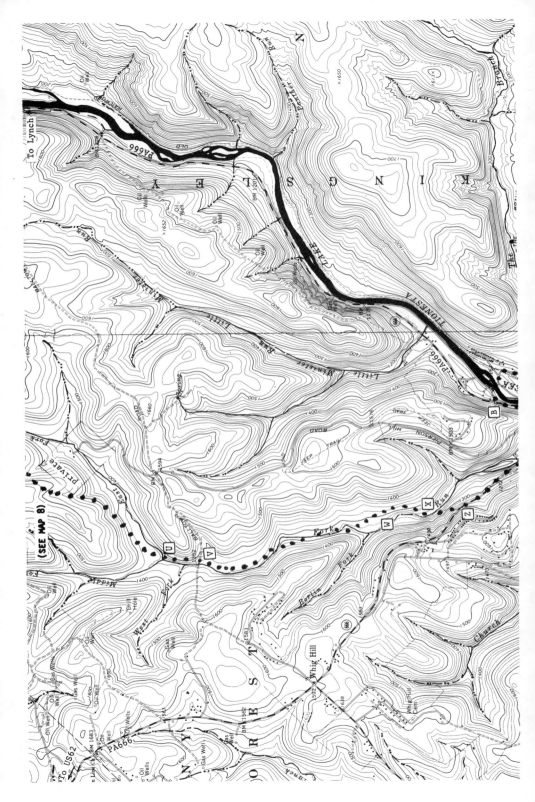

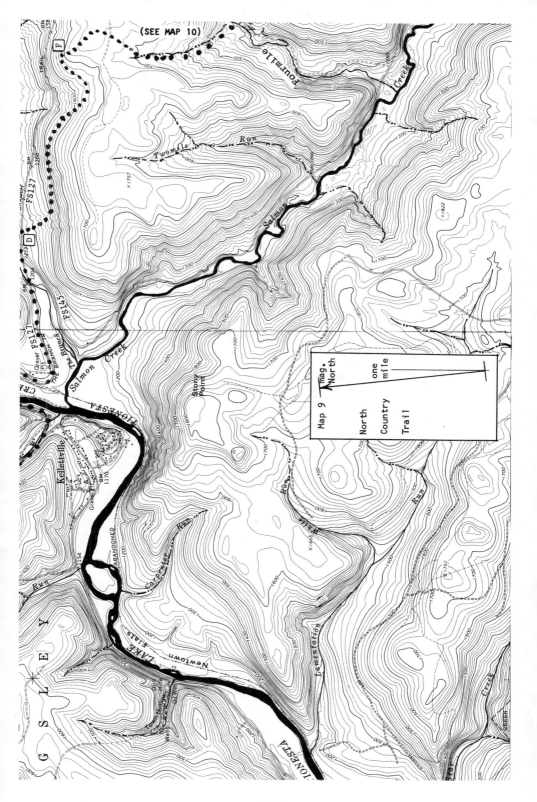

(SEE MAP 10)

Map 9

Mag.
North

one
mile

North
Country
Trail

Rock ledge along the North Country Trail between Kellettville
and the Baker Trail. Photo by Helen Marquard.

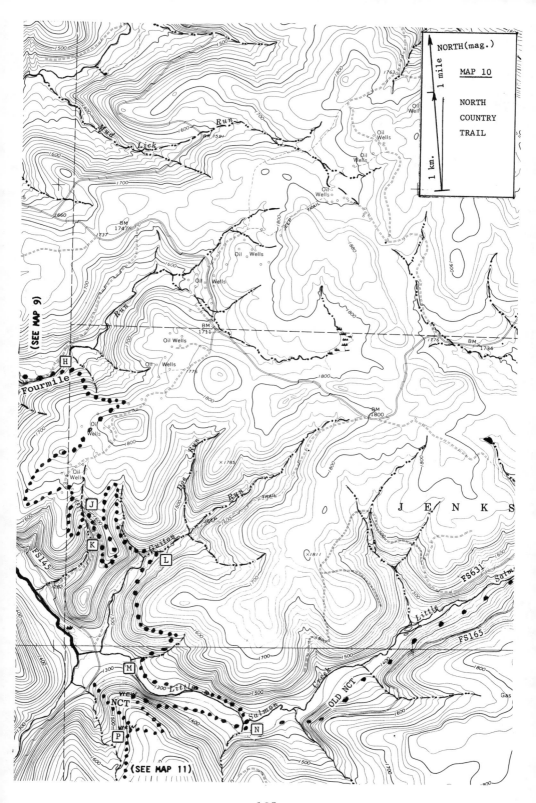

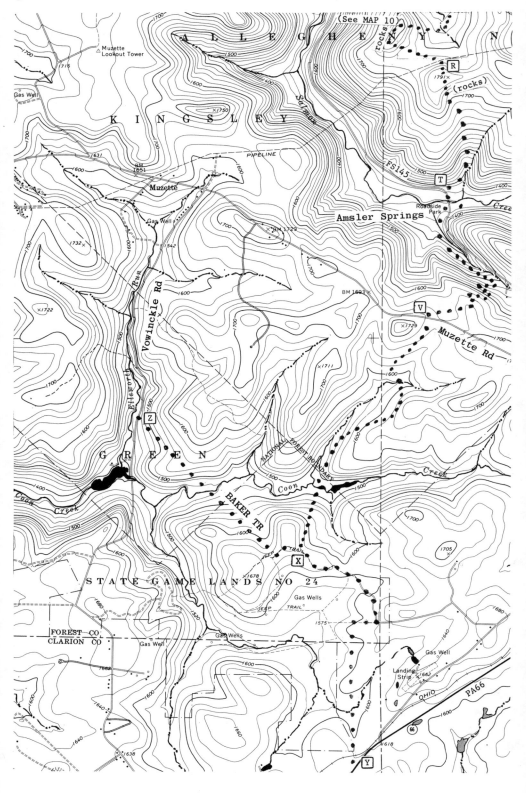

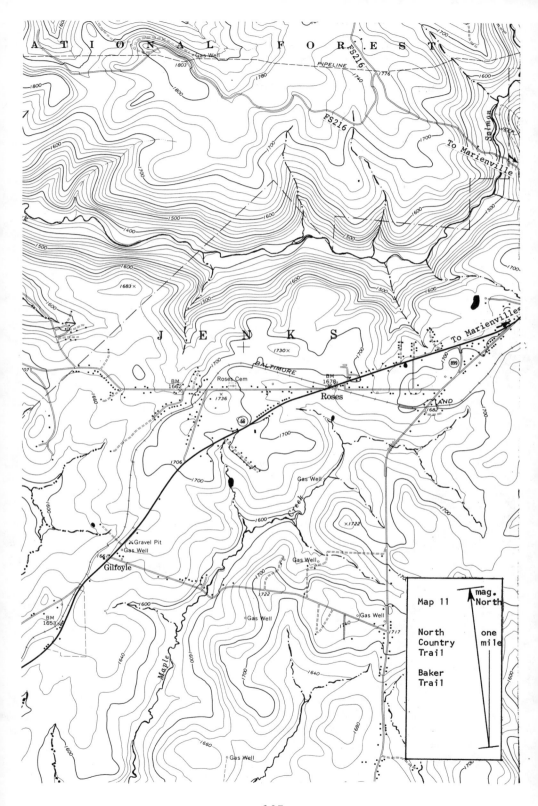

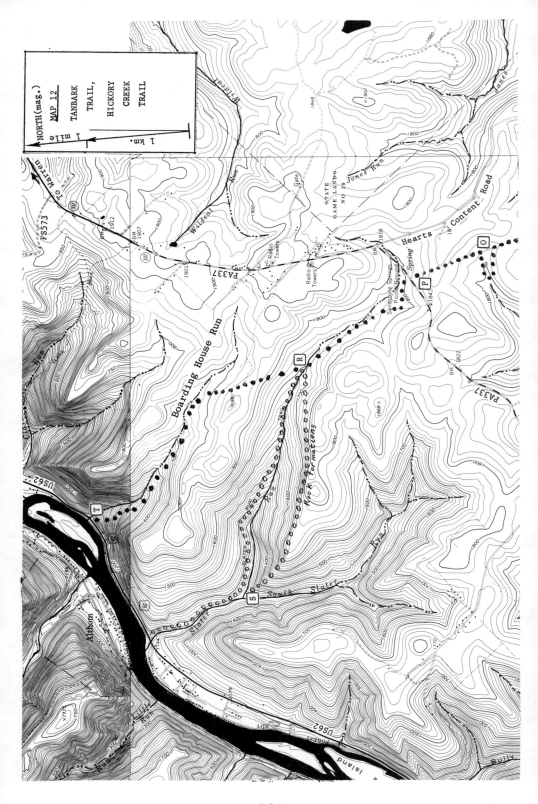

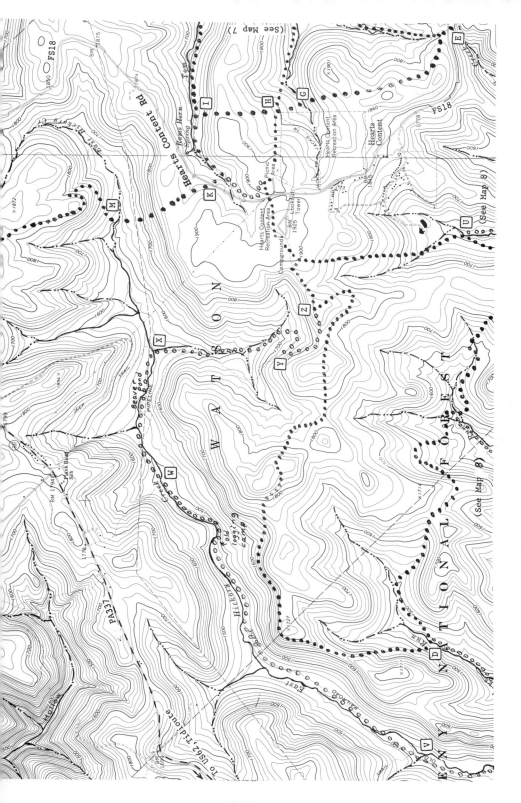

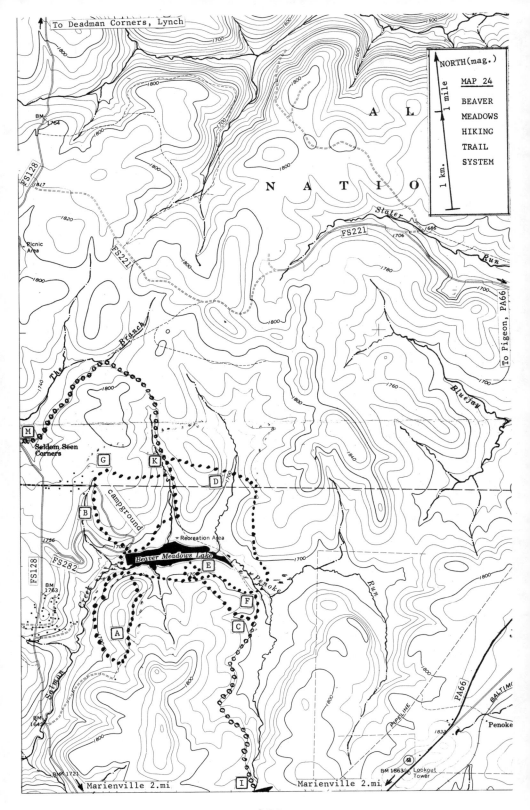

To Deadman Corners, Lynch

NORTH(mag.)

MAP 24

BEAVER
MEADOWS
HIKING
TRAIL
SYSTEM

1 mile

1 km.

A L

N A T I O

N A T I O

Stater

FS221

To Pigeon, PA66

Bluejay

FS128

Picnic
Area

The Branch

Seldom Seen
Corners

M

G

K

D

B

campground

Recreation Area

Beaver Meadows Lake

FS282

FS128

E

Penoke

Run

F

A

C

Salmon Creek

PA66

BALTIMO

PIPELINE

Penoke

BM 1863

68

Lookout
Tower

BM 1721

Marienville 2.mi

I

Marienville 2.mi

Starting out from Sandstone Spring for a hike in the Allegheny
Front Area.

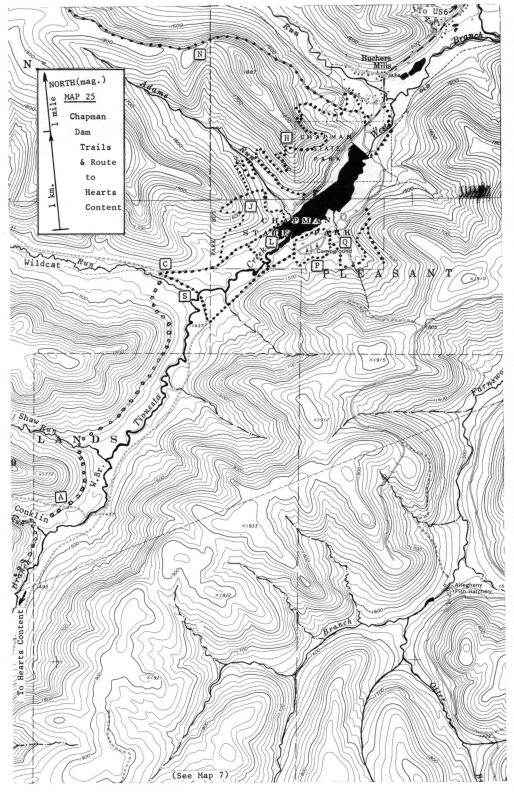

TRAILS OF SOUTHEASTERN ALLEGHENY
NATIONAL FOREST

The boundary separating the southeastern region of the ANF from the northern region in this guide is US6. The boundary between the southwestern and southeastern ANF, for purposes of this guide, is as follows:

PA948 between Sheffield (on US6) and Barnes:
PA666 between Barnes and Lynch;
LR1003 between Lynch and Pigeon (on PA66),
PA66 from Pigeon to Marienville.

LR1003 is also known as the Blue Jay Trail. (It runs along Blue Jay Creek.) Some USFS maps label PA948 between Sheffield and Barnes as PA666.

In the southeastern region of the ANF the hiker finds three clusters of trails. In the northern part of the region one finds:

- Sections 4 and 5 of the North Country Trail
- Twin Lakes Trail
- Black Cherry Interpretive Trail
- Mill Creek Trail
- Upper Bear Creek Trail

All of these trails, except Upper Bear Creek Trail, are formal (USFS-maintained) trails. Black Cherry and Mill Creek are loop trails. In the southeastern part of the region one finds:

- Lower Bear Creek Trail
- Clarion River Trail
- Laurel Mill Ski/Hiking Trail
- Irwin Run Trail
- Big Run Trail
- Pigeon Run Falls Trail

Of these trails, only Laurel Mill Ski/Hiking Trail is a formal USFS trail. The rest are not maintained by the USFS, not blazed and not maintained. They are thus more subject to wind/ice storms making portions non-negotiable. For the most part, they follow old logging RR grades built early in this century. So experienced hikers should find it easy to follow them. In the SW portion of the region (near Marienville) one finds:

- Buzzard Swamp Wildlife Management Area
- Loleta Hiking Trail (loop)
- Songbird Sojourn Interpretive Trail (loop)
- Buzzard Swamp Ski-touring Loop Trails System

All these trails are formal (USFS-maintained) trails. The Buzzard Swamp Wildlife Management Area is not a trail in the formal sense, but a variety of woods roads that are primarily of interest to people interested in viewing the wildlife that the Buzzard Swamp Area is noted for.

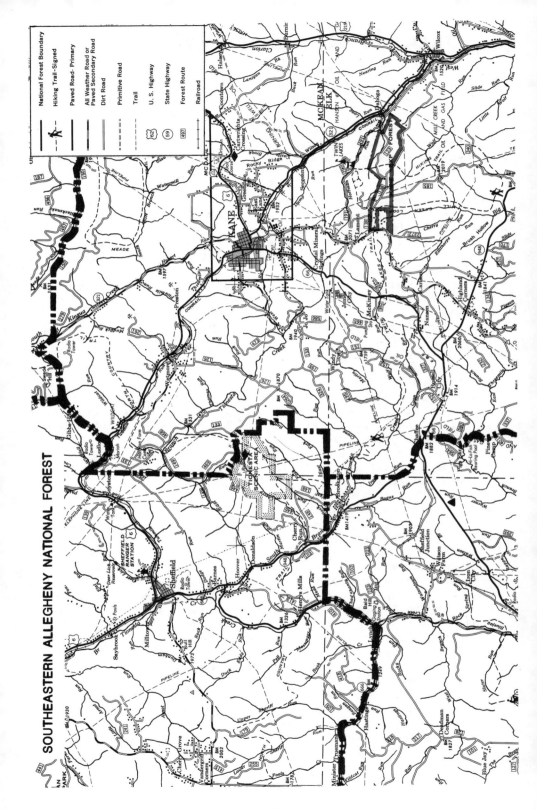

SOUTHEASTERN ALLEGHENY NATIONAL FOREST

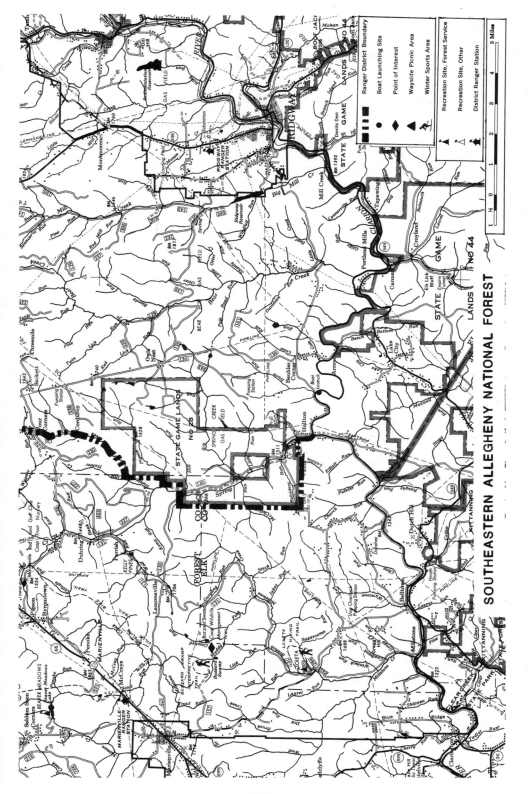

SOUTHEASTERN ALLEGHENY NATIONAL FOREST

A prime scenic attraction of the southeastern region of
the ANF is the Clarion River. A significant portion of the
banks of the Clarion are in public ownership--national forest,
state gamelands and state parks. Portions of the Clarion River
may some day be protected as a National Scenic- or Recreational
River. The Clarion River drainage covers the SE quarter of
Allegheny National Forest. Despite these considerations, the
USFS seems to have paid inadequate attention to the development
of formal (USFS) trails in the drainage. As a result, various
individuals have scouted out several informal trails that per-
mit one to enjoy at least two of the prime scenic attractions
of that portion of the Forest--Clarion River and Bear Creek.
These trails are described below. Three of them form a loop
that offers an ideal route for a three-day backpacking trip.

NCT SECTION 4,   US6 TO TIONESTA SCENIC AREA   5.2mi(8.4km)
SCEN: 1   DIFF: II   COND: A
SKI-: S4   NOTE: B,M,O   ELEV: 1910/1480
MAPS: Ludlow, USFS(A), Maps 4 and 5 in this Guide
TRAIL SEGMENTS:
 (1) US6   to FS133   1.8mi
 (2) FS133 to FS149   0.7mi
 (3) FS149 to FS133E (Tionesta Scenic Area) 2.7mi

The main attractions of this section of the NCT are the
Tionesta Scenic Area and the Tionesta Research Natural Area.
Together they represent one of the largest stands of virgin
forest in the eastern U.S.--six square miles. Unfortunately
1/3 of the trees in Tionesta Scenic Area were lost in a May 31,
1985 tornado. The forest is typical of what once covered all
of northern Pennsylvania. The trees are mainly sugar maple,
hemlock, beech, and yellow birch. Black Cherry, red maple,
white ash, and black birch are also seen. In 1973, both the
Scenic Area and the Research Natural Area were added to the
National Registry of Natural Landmarks Program in recognition
of their unique characteristics.
Camping is not permitted in either the Scenic Area or the
Research Natural Area.
In addition to the NCT, two shorter foot trails are found
in the Tionesta Scenic Area. One is 1.0mi long; the other is
0.25mi long. Both begin from a common point near the parking
area on the access road (FS133E). They are blue-blazed and
connect to the NCT. They are not described in this Guide.
As of September, 1989, this section is well maintained and
clean. Blazes are clearly visible and recently repainted.
Access: Signs mark where the NCT crosses US6 (G ,Map 4), 2.mi
E of Ludlow. Ample parking is found in the area. The S trailhead is 0.2mi off FS133 on a side road (FS133E) leading into
Tionesta Scenic Area. The trailhead is signed. Parking is lim-

ited. At Wetmore Road $\boxed{\text{I}}$ (paved)(0.5mi S of US6) parking is
marginal, but this crossing is signed.
     To get to the S trailhead, turn off PA66 near the S edge
of Kane onto JoJo Road. Follow JoJo Road to a "Y" (signed).
Take the left branch (FS133) and drive 6.mi to the Tionesta
Scenic- and Research-Natural Areas. To get to Tionesta Scenic
Area from US6 and Ludlow, drive 7.mi S from Ludlow on FS133.
Segment 1: From US6 $\boxed{\text{G}}$, the NCT heads SW, dropping down to a
foot bridge across Twomile Run. From there, climb up to a RR
track, cross it, and continue climbing through pine wood.
Cross Wetmore Road $\boxed{\text{I}}$. Proceed NW, crossing a few woods
roads, to a telephone-line swath at top of the hill (1865').
Turn left (NW) down the swath. After 500yd along the swath,
turn left (W) $\boxed{\text{K}}$ into woods before reaching another hill top.
Drop SW down the ridge, crossing a large pipeline swath. Continue the descent past a large rock ledge to FS133 $\boxed{\text{L}}$.
Segment 2: Cross FS133 and turn S down the valley (a tributary
of East Branch of Tionesta Creek), crossing the stream twice
before staying on the E bank. A large clearcut is visible
across the stream. Apart from nearby FS133, it is a nice
stretch of trail, with hemlock and large rock blocks. The
trail emerges on FS149 $\boxed{\text{M}}$ just E of the bridge over East
Branch of Tionesta Creek. FS149 and the bridge are gated to
vehicle traffic. North-bound hikers should take note: one must
cross the bridge and enter the trail in a NNE direction. The
cut for a new road has obscured the trail entrance.
Segment 3: Turn right (W) and cross the FS149 bridge, then
turn left (SE) into an attractive grove of hemlocks along East
Branch of Tionesta Creek. After 0.5mi, cross a RR grade $\boxed{\text{N}}$ on
the right (S) and climb a hill with a switch-back near the top
(1680'). Join an old RR grade and go SE around the E end of
the ridge. Descend 100ft and climb gradually S along the W
side of a side stream valley through hemlocks, grassy bottoms
and some rock blocks. Cross roads, a new well, and pipeline
swaths, as shown on the topo. \Map 5\. After several crossings of small streams at the head of the drainage, climb SE to
FS133E $\boxed{\text{P}}$ which leads W into the Tionesta Scenic Area $\boxed{\text{Q}}$.

NCT SEC.5   TIONESTA SCENIC AREA TO HENRYS MILLS   10.1mi(16.3km)

SCEN: 1	DIFF: II	COND: A
SKI-: S4	NOTE: B,M,1	ELEV: 1970/1300

MAPS: Ludlow, Sheffield, USFS(A), Maps 5 and 6 in this Guide
TRAIL SEGMENTS:
  (1) FS133E to Twin Lakes Trail   3.3mi
  (2) Twin Lakes Trail to PA948   3.0mi
  (3) PA948 to Henrys Mills (PA666)   3.8mi

     The first few miles of trail at the N end of this section
run through Tionesta Scenic Area (3.3sq.mi) which contains lots
of virgin timber. Immediately SE of the Scenic Area is the

3.1sq.mi Tionesta Research Natural Area which contains no
trails and is used for research, studying the changes that
occur in an old-growth forest.
Access: The N trailhead is 100yd off FS133E (P ,Map 5) into
the Tionesta Scenic Area, 0.2mi off FS133. The trailhead is
signed. Parking is limited. At PA948 (X ,Map 5) the trail is
well signed and parking is ample near the bridge over Tionesta
Creek, but meager on PA948. At the S trailhead (A ,Map 6) one
can park at the S end of the PA666 bridge over Tionesta Creek.
Segment 1: Due to the May 1985 tornado, the bulk of Segment 1
was rerouted. The new trail starts about 100yd N of FS133E P
and heads W. It is blazed with white plastic strips. At 1.3mi
the NCT intersects an old interpretive trail. A sign on a
badly chewed post says "North Country Trail", "Scenic Loop" and
"End of Loop". This section of trail passes through some very
large and beautiful trees. The trail then turns S at a pipeline Q and passes through the heart of the 1985 tornado
destruction. (1.4sq.mi of Tionesta Scenic Area was destroyed.)
Walking through this area can be an awesome experience. Cross
Cherry Run and continue S on the pipeline corridor as it climbs
out of Cherry Run Valley and reconnects with the original route
of the NCT at 2.7mi. Turn W and then bear SW and cross a road
S . Reach the junction with the W end of blue-blazed Twin
Lakes Trail T .
Segment 2: Shortly after leaving Twin Lakes Trail, recross the
dirt road U mentioned above and enter the woods. Soon you'll
pass several large rock blocks. (If you plan to camp in the
area, camp along Cherry Run above the 1500ft. level V as it
gets marshy in the lower reaches. Note: camping must be done
outside the boundaries of the Tionesta Scenic/Research Area).
Follow an old woods road that crosses several old pipelines and
descends into Cherry Run. Pass the boundary (display case)
marker of the Tionesta Scenic Area. Cross Cherry Run on fallen
timber at an OGM site V . Soon, recross the stream on pipes
amid old OGM activity. Climb SW, away from the stream and
cross a power line shown on the topo. Join a lower old road
from the right and return to the stream. OGM sites and pipelines are common here, but the stream is attractive. Cross
Cherry Run again, passing the remains of an old RR caboose.
Continue 0.1mi futher to pass a spring flowing from a pipe.
After another 0.1mi, the trail joins an old road for 30yd
before turning left to follow Cherry Run. The trail intersects
FS446 30yd from the bridge over Tionesta Creek. FS148 and the
bridge over Tionesta Creek are visible at this point. Proceed
W over the South Branch of Tionesta Creek. Just after the
FS148/FS446 bridge the trail leaves the road and heads NW along
the South Branch of Tionesta Creek, through a nice hemlock
woods. After 0.3mi reach PA948 X .
Segment 3: Cross PA948, climb a short distance and travel parallel to PA948 through the woods. Leaving PA948 out of sight,
the NCT heads W through the woods, crosses to the N side of

FS103 and continues W through an OGM area up an unnamed creek valley. Recross to the S bank [Z] of the stream and follow the valley NW, gradually climbing up an old OGM road to the hill top. \Map 6\. At the woods road [A], turn left (W). This area contains a maze of woods roads, but the trail route is well-blazed. Some jogs avoid clearcuts, but the trend is generally S, down the ridge. Cross FS413 (not signed) and descend into an unnamed stream valley, crossing two pipeline swaths on the way. The trail bears NW around the flank of a hill on a woods road, and joins paved Henrys Mills Road [D]. The trail is signed on the road. Turn left (SSW) and head downhill, paralleling a tributary on the right (W). Emerge at Henrys Mills, between a house and a garage, at the N end of the bridge carrying PA666 over Tionesta Creek.

<u>TWIN LAKES TRAIL</u>   15.9mi(25.6km)
SCEN: 2   DIFF: II   COND: A (except(4)=C)
SKI-: S4   NOTE: B,M,7   ELEV: 2040/1450
MAPS: James City, Russell City, Ludlow, USFS(A), Maps, 15, 14
and 5 in this Guide
TRAIL SEGMENTS:
  (1) Twin Lakes Recreation Area to FS31(Lamont Rd.) 2.3mi
  (2) FS31 (Lamont Road) to PA66   2.3mi
  (3) PA66 to FS152   3.0mi
  (4) FS152 to NCT   .   8.3mi
      (NCT to Tionesta Scenic Area via NCT   1.9mi)

     Twin Lakes Trail extends W from the Twin Lakes Recreation Area, SE of Kane, to connect with the NCT near the Tionesta Scenic/Natural Area.
<u>Access</u>: At the E trailhead the trail begins as the Black Cherry Trail ([A],Map 15) on the W side of FS191, 300yd N of the turn-off to the beach and administration building in the Twin Lakes Recreation Area. Parking is available near the administration building. Camping is also available. At PA66 the trailhead is signed and offers parking for 4 cars. A trail sign marks the crossing of FS152 where parking is available.
<u>Segment 1</u>: Starting from the E, Twin Lakes Trail begins as the Black Cherry Trail, a nature-interpretation trail in the Recreation Area. Leave FS191, heading SW. After 0.7mi, the beginning of the Twin Lakes Trail proper is signed at the T-junction [Z]. Turn right onto the trail. Follow a grassy woods road, then climb uphill, cross a dirt road, and continue along the hillside. Reach FS331 [C] at a telephone line; cross and continue until you cross FS331 again (not signed). Reach FS138 [D] just E of its junction with FS191. A sign reads: "Lamont Rd. 0.7, PA66 2.7, Black Cherry Trail 1.3mi". Cross FS138, heading S, but soon turn W. Pass Stone Camp shown on the topo near where Mill Creek Loop Trail departs to the S. Travel W on an old grade and cross a RR track just before reaching paved Lamont Road [E] (SR-24006). Trail signs are seen here.

Lush fern carpet along Twin Lakes Trail.   Photo by Carolyn Yartz.

Segment 2: Head W from Lamont Road and descend into the upper valley of Wolf Run. The trail jogs left (S) at a large grassy pipe-line swath. After this jog, follow the old RR grade as it gradually descends along the stream. Cross to the S bank of Wolf Run $\boxed{G}$. Climb away from the stream to a vista and drop SSW down to PA66 $\boxed{I}$.

Segment 3: Cross PA66 at the bridge. Head W, gradually climbing SW. (The former trail route--a pipeline and an old RR grade near the stream--has been abandoned due to tornado damage.) Continue W to the top of the plateau crossing a logging road. Two "tornado swath" overlooks are maintained near the edge of the damaged timber. Watch for signs. Head SW, cross a pipeline and timber road to an old RR grade at the headwaters of Coon Run. Turn left (S). Arrive at the junction with Old NCT $\boxed{K}$. Blue-blazed Twin Lake Trail turns right (W) here. Straight ahead is the Old NCT (now an ATV trail). (To reach PA66, continue along Old NCT S, crossing a small stream and a pipeline. Climb, cross a RR tracks and, after 0.5mi from the trail junction $\boxed{K}$, reach PA66 at Nansen, W of a RR crossing. Parking is meagre on PA66.)

Continue on Twin Lakes Trail from the junction with Old NCT. Follow the N bank of Coon Run W \Map 14\ on a RR grade in young timber. Pass an old beaver pond ($\boxed{L}$,Map 14). Cross Coon Run on a pole bridge at a pipeline swath $\boxed{M}$. Leave the RR grade and climb out of Coon Run valley through OGM activity reaching FS152 $\boxed{N}$ where there is a trail sign.

Segment 4: The trail for the next 1.8mi has been rerouted around tornado damage. Go 200yd N along FS152 and turn left (WNW) down an old woods road. (The trail is signed at the turn.) Follow this woods road 1.6mi and turn left, uphill, to intersect the old trail route. This route continues W and crosses a power line swath. Beyond the swath is a fine spring near a stand of hemlock. Cross Coon Run on a log $\boxed{R}$ and pass the junction with Tionesta Creek near an open field. The trail follows a logging road down the S side of the valley of South Branch of Tionesta Creek. Cross South Branch of Tionesta Creek $\boxed{S}$ where a pipeline swath crosses. About 100yd up the swath, turn left (NW) and proceed along the N bank of the creek. Then climb the hillside, crossing another swath, and go through hemlock and pine. \Map 5\ Camping is possible near Crane Run.

Cross Crane Run where a power line swath (shown on the topo) intersects. Go into the woods N of the swath, but then cross back over the swath; the trail then parallels the swath. Cross a side stream and zig-zag uphill ($\boxed{C}$,Map 5). Reach a dirt road on the ridge top (not shown on topo). Follow a logging road; recross the power line swath at East Fork Run $\boxed{E}$ on stepping stones. A good campsite is found here in a flat field. Climb N to the ridge top and drop to West Fork Run on an old logging road. An attractive lunch spot with hemlock is found here. Climb steeply (NW) to the road $\boxed{G}$ at the boundary

of Tionesta Natural Area. Twin Lakes Trail proceeds along the
ridge (NNE) to the North Country Trail T .
    Follow the NCT N for 1.9mi to the Tionesta Scenic Area
access road FS133E P .

BLACK CHERRY TRAIL   1.6mi(2.6km)
SKI-: S1   NOTE: I,M,0   ELEV: 1850/1750
MAPS: James City, USFS(A), Map 15 in this Guide
TRAIL SEGMENTS:
 (1) FS191 to FS191 (Twin Lakes Rec. Area)   1.6mi

    Black Cherry Trail is a National Trail. It also serves as
the N end of Mill Creek Loop Trail and as the E end of Twin
Lakes Trail. It is an interpretive trail, with 36 interpretive
stops which depict unique and interesting aspects of the
"Forest Community". It is meant to serve as an easy walk for
all age groups. A shorter loop cuts off half way through the
main trail, allowing a shorter hike for those not wishing to
hike the complete trail. It is in the Ridgway Ranger District.
Access: The Black Cherry Trail begins and ends in the lower
loop of the Twin Lakes Camping Area.
Segment 1: The route is easy to follow and the treadway is
well-worn. Directions for following the trail are not needed.

MILL CREEK (LOOP) TRAIL   16.7mi(26.9km)
SCEN: 2   DIFF: II   COND: A
SKI-: S4   NOTE: B,M,6   ELEV: 2060/1630
MAPS: James City, Wilcox, USFS(A), Maps 15, 16 and 19 in this
      Guide
TRAIL SEGMENTS:
 (1) Twin Lakes Rec. Area (FS191) to Twin Lakes Trail D   2.1mi
 (2) Twin Lakes Trail D to cross-trail X   2.9mi
 (3) cross-trail to near PA948 A   2.0mi
 (4) Near PA948 to cross-trail T   5.4mi
 (5) cross-trail to Twin Lakes Rec. Area (FS191)   4.2mi
     (Total short (upper) loop= 10.5mi= (1)+(2)+(5)+1.3mi)

    In 1978 the USFS opened three new loop foot trails on the
ANF. One of these was Mill Creek Trail. The portion of Mill
Creek Trail along Big Mill Creek is easily followed and would
make an excellent ski-touring route. Mill Creek Trail connects
with Twin Lakes Trail (See p.139.) and with Bear Creek Trail
(See p.144.), so that a number of hiking- and back-packing
options are available. Numerous pleasant grassy jeep trails
intersect all of these trails for those who prefer exploratory-
type hiking. Many areas of open, fern-carpeted woodlands,
devoid of brushy under-story, also invite exploratory hiking.
Allow time for side trips and stopping to enjoy the scenery.
The Ridgway Ranger District (814-776-6172) is in charge of Mill

Creek Trail. Mill Creek Trail is composed of two loops, so
that two one-day hikes and a leisurely backpacking trip are
possible. The entire trail is blazed with yellow paint and is
easy to follow.

Some areas along Mill Creek Trail will be undergoing logging operations during 1989-1991. So hikers should contact the
Ridgway District Ranger's office (See above and page 25) for
current trail conditions and/or closings. According to the
Ridgway District Ranger, once timber cutting is completed,
trail traffic will be shifted to a permanent site where timber
management activities have been minimized. Vistas and other
special viewing areas will be included. By 1993 the Mill Creek
Loop Trail should be joined with the new Cherry Mill Trail. It
will have a multi-purpose designation of hiking and ski-touring
with historical interpretation at certain sites. These trails
are in a special management area designated in the Forest Plan.
By 1996 all motorized activity will be terminated. Except for
oil and gas management, all road use will be halted and ORVs
will be excluded from the area. This quiet condition will be
enforced and no timber harvesting will be practiced for 30
years.

Access: This trail is most conveniently accessed at Twin Lakes
Recreation (Camping) Area. One could also easily access it via
PA948 just E of the PA948 Bridge over Big Mill Creek or off
FS185 from PA948.

Segment 1: Start out near [A](Map 15), the W edge of the lake
at Twin Lakes Recreation Area. A sign here says "Black Cherry
Trail, Twin Lakes Trail 0.7mi". Follow this (unblazed) Black
Cherry Trail W to Twin Lakes Trail [Z]. This trail junction is
signed. The sign marking blue-blazed Twin-Lakes Trail says
"FS138 1.3mi, Lamont Road 2mi, PA66 4mi, N. Country Trail 6mi".
Follow Twin Lakes Trail W 1.3mi to FS138 [D].

Segment 2: Mill Creek Trail leaves Twin Lakes Trail [D] on the
S side of FS138 and heads S. A sign at this trail junction
points back toward Twin Lakes (1.5mi) and another sign says
"Mill Creek Trail - Long Loop 13.5mi, Short Loop 7.5mi". Follow yellow-blazed Mill Creek Trail S through a fern-carpeted
cherry-maple forest.

Segment 3: At [X] Mill Creek Trail branches at a signed intersection. A sign pointing down the E branch (cross trail) says
"Short Loop, Twin Lakes 5". The sign pointing down the S
branch says "Mill Creek Trail, Twin Lakes 11". The E branch is
the cut-off that provides the 10.5-mile short loop. It rejoins
the main loop [T] after 1.3mi. This cut-off offers no particular scenic value and is easily followed. It is not described
further here. NOTE: The cut-off ([X] to [T]) is closed (1989-
1990) due to logging operations. The description below continues with the main 16.7mi "Long Loop".

From the trail junction [X], the S branch drops down-hill
to a wide, grassy jeep trail along Big Mill Creek. Grassy
meadows and stands of young hemlock and red pine make this por-

tion of the trail picturesque. Hikers wanting to get to Bear
Creek Trail [Y] should watch for opportunities to cross Big
Mill Creek within 0.5mi of the above-mentioned junction. At
least be sure to cross upstream of Ellithorpe Run. Watch carefully for the point ([A],Map 16) where the blazed Mill Creek
Trail leads E, away from the unblazed trail that continues S
along Big Mill Creek for 0.2mi to PA948.
Segment 4: After leaving Big Mill Creek [A] the trail travels
along old RR grades, old woods roads and around timber harvest
areas. In the vicinity of FS185 and Little Mill Creek [C] the
surroundings are especially picturesque. The last 1.5mi before
the junction [T](Map 15) with the cross trail is scenic. At [V]
is a vista overlooking an area of tornado damage and timber
salvage. An information board is located here. At the trail
junction [T] are USFS trail signs. The sign on the short loop
says "Twin Lakes 5mi"). The other sign says "Mill Creek Trail,
Twin Lakes 11mi" (pointing E) and "Twin Lakes, 4mi" (Pointing
N).
Segment 5: Continuing N along the long loop, the forest is
particularly pleasant E of the Kane Experimental Forest headquarters (black cherry and beech). At the junction [Q] with
FS191 is a USFS sign pointing back the way you came and saying
"Mill Creek Trail, Short Loop 9mi, Long Loop 15mi".

UPPER BEAR CREEK TRAIL   10.2mi(16.4km)
SCEN: 2   DIFF: II   COND: C
SKI: S1   NOTE: B,M,14   ELEV: 1910/1450
MAPS: James City, Portland Mills, USFS(A), Maps 15, 16 and 17
      in this Guide
TRAIL SEGMENTS:
  (1) Bear Creek Picnic Area to PA948   7.5mi
  (2) PA948 to Mill Creek Loop Trail   2.7mi

     Bear Creek runs N to S through public lands for virtually
its entire length. It empties into the Clarion River across
from Portland Mills. Few clearcuts, gas wells, pipelines, etc.
mar Bear Creek's scenery. Some scenic savannahs (broad, open
meadows with scattered trees) also make the area excellent for
hiking and back-packing. Because Bear Creek must be waded several times, Bear Creek Trail should be avoided during spring
runoffs. Also, the open meadows make the trail less pleasant
than other ANF trails in mid-summer. May, June, September and
October are the best times to visit Bear Creek Trail.
     Bear Creek Trail follows the route of a long-abandoned RR
grade which ran the entire length of Bear Creek. Bear Creek
Trail joins Big Run Trail at Red Lick Run, 0.8mi N of Bear
Creek Picnic Area. It also joins the Clarion River Trail near
where Bear Creek empties into the Clarion River. Irwin Run
Trail makes possible a 3-day backpack trip utilizing Lower Bear
Creek Trail as one leg of a triangular loop. PA948 to Bear

The rock dam across Bear Creek at the Bear Creek Picnic Area
(part of Bear Creek Trail). Photo by Carolyn Yartz.

Creek Picnic Area makes an excellent day hike. Twin Lakes Campground to Bear Creek Picnic Area (using part of Mill Creek Trail) makes a pleasant weekend backpack trip. Good campsites are easy to find along the entire route.

Access: Ample parking is available for cars along FS237 just off PA948. Do not park along PA948. Ample parking is also available in the Bear Creek Picnic Area.

Segment 1: Starting from Bear Creek Picnic Area (A ,Map 17), locate a stone dam across Bear Creek, forming a small pond. Cross to the E side of Bear Creek on this dam. (One could also cross at a bridge 0.1mi downstream.) Turn N and cross Bloody Run close to its junction with Bear Creek. You will then quickly find an old (grassy) RR grade which you will be following for most of the rest of the trip. Do not confuse it with a dirt jeep trail (shown on the topo) a few yards uphill from the RR grade. For the next 2.mi Bear Creek Trail follows close to Bear Creek on its E bank. Note a small open meadow (and slightly obscure trail) at B and a footbridge over Bear Creek just downstream of the mouth of Red Lick Run and at C . The last 0.3mi before the junction with Twin Lick Run is a grassy jeep trail in a broad meadow.

At the junction with Twin Lick Run is a large informal car-camp site. Cross the car bridge to the W bank of Bear Creek. Then turn N again and cross a small metal foot-bridge over Twin Lick Run. There you will see a pleasant jeep trail paralleling Bear Creek. \Map 16\ Walk N 0.7mi to the intersection E with the first obvious gas line swath (also used as a jeep trail). Turn E and go down to Bear Creek and wade across to the E bank. Continue E 30yd through an open area to a dirt jeep trail. Turn N and continue on, parallel to Bear Creek. Note the signs and a one-wire fence that forbids fishing in a small portion of Bear Creek 50 yd upstream of where you waded. You are now on the James City Topo map. At F is a scenic marsh with an island of trees in the middle. Much wildlife is seen in this area. About 100yd past the marsh your jeep trail branches. Avoid the right (E) branch. In wet weather continue straight ahead. In drier weather take the left (W) branch down to a popular informal campsite along Bear Creek G . Turn N and walk through open, fern-carpeted forest (no trail), keeping 10yd from Bear Creek. After 0.3mi rejoin the jeep road where it fords Bear Creek H . Wade across to the W bank. The trail is now a grassy jeep trail through a broad meadow with scattered trees.

Cross Maple Run, avoiding the side trail up Maple Run (though it may be interesting to explore). Note the old stumps of the giant trees that once covered these meadows. It is probable that when the area was cut the water table rose because of a lack of trees to transpire the water away. As a result, further tree growth was inhibited. Normally trees would grow slowly back into the meadow from the edge. But this has probably been inhibited, in part, by the excess deer popu-

lation. Note the deer fence around the clear-cut up on the
hillside between Maple Run and Pigeon Run.

The 2 miles N of Pigeon Run have a number of stream crossings, and the trail can be slightly obscure in spots. A power
line corridor is crossed 1.0mi N of Pigeon Run. There are many
meadows. At [J] is a scenic stream crossing in a dense stand
of hemlock. Just N of this crossing is a clear-cut dating back
to around 1980. The old RR grade approximately skirts the E
edge of this impenetrable cut. Follow the old RR grade carefully along the clearcut. It gets obscure in a few spots. Not
far N of the N end of the clearcut [K] leave the Bear Creek RR
grade (in order to stay on public property) and go E up a side-
stream, with large exposed rocks in its 4-5ft. bed, to FS237
near its junction with PA948. There is no continuous trail
along this side-stream of Bear Creek. However the woods are
open and offer easy walking. When the topography gets flat and
the stream-bed becomes obscure use your compass to stay on
course.

Segment 2: The function of this trail segment is to join Bear
Creek Trail to Mill Creek (loop) Trail, a formal USFS hiking
trail. If one is merely seeking to hike from Twin Lakes Campground to PA948 it would probably be preferable to hike along
Mill Creek Trail all the way to the PA948 bridge, where cars
can be spotted.

NOTE: This area is closed for 1990-1991 due to timber harvest
activities. See the introduction to Mill Creek Trail on page
for information from the Ridgway District Ranger on future
plans.

On reaching PA948 turn E and walk along PA948 for 0.2mi to
gated FS491 [M] where a jeep trail turns N off PA948. Follow
this road over a small hill to an old oil well site. Note the
ancient spring house (and spring and dam) beside the trail just
beyond the well site. Continue NNE to a T intersection [N].
The SE branch is a non-descript dirt jeep trail of no particular interest. The NW branch (unscouted) doubtlessly leads
across a saddle to the old RR grade along Ellithorpe Run which
is pleasant hiking (at least along its scouted lower end). The
NW branch and the Ellithorpe RR grade is the recommended route.

Upon reaching the junction [P] of Ellithorpe Run and Big
Mill Creek (via either route) turn N on a pleasant grassy trail
along Big Mill Creek. Walk at least as far as Cherry Run.
([Y], Map 15) Then cross Big Mill Creek (no trail or bridge)
to join Mill Creek Trail (yellow blazes) a short walk to the E
of Big Mill Creek.

Old beaver dam along Bear Creek and Bear Creek Trail. Photo by Carolyn Yartz.

LOWER BEAR CREEK TRAIL   6.5mi(10.5km)
SCEN: 2   DIFF: II   COND: C
SKI-: S4   NOTE: B,M,4   ELEV: 1450/1320
MAPS: Portland Mills, USFS(A), Maps 17 and 18 in this Guide
TRAIL SEGMENTS:
  (1) Bear Creek Picnic Area to T-307   6.5mi

Access: Bear Creek Picnic Area offers ample parking off
FS135.1. At T-307 (formerly FS20) is parking for 4-5 cars in a
fisherman's parking lot (Q ,Map 18) on the W side of Bear
Creek on the N side of T-307.
Segment 1: Starting from the N and Bear Creek Picnic Area, A
(Map 17), Bear Creek Trail starts out on the W side of the
creek as a fisherman's trail. (Bear Creek is a popular trout
stream.) (Hikers coming S from PA948 on the E side of Bear
Creek should cross to the W side on the FS135.1 bridge, 0.1mi S
of the picnic area, or else cross the stone dam at the picnic
area.) After 0.1mi cross FS135.1 and continue on a stream-side
fisherman's trail. At E scramble 5yd up a steep hillside to
a narrow, grassy jeep trail. Take this S 0.15mi to F , a
gasline swath down to Bear Creek. Cross the creek. On the E
bank of Bear Creek is the old RR grade that is the basis of
Bear Creek Trail. Take this grade S through non-descript woodlands and a few small open stream-side meadows to G opposite
Italian Shanty Run.
      From G to H are more open meadows and marshlands. The
RR grade is elevated somewhat above the flood plane. At H
the old grade crosses Bear Creek twice, but no trace of the old
bridges remain. One can easily follow a deer trail around to
the E of this double crossing if desired. From H to Little
Otter Creek the trail is clearly defined. For the next 1.0mi S
of Little Otter Creek are many outstanding views of the huge
open meadows and marshlands to the W. At J cross a deep
ravine (once traversed by a bridge). In the vicinity of Shanty
Run is evidence of beaver among the Aspen groves. Just below
Shanty Run is a nice campsite.
      At a large pipeline corridor K look for a place to rock-
hop across to the W bank of Bear Creek. The sometimes obscure
old RR grade continues S along the W side of Bear Creek--some-
times as much as 50yd from the stream bed. At L is a sizeable beaver dam. After 0.8mi from K the trail once again becomes obvious at an old RR grade M . Between M and N
the trail is especially pleasant with frequent hemlock groves.
At N is a rock dam that could be used to cross the creek.
(Various trails on the E bank lead N to K .) A short distance
below N is a broad power-line corridor. Davidson Run, O , a
short distance S is an attractive side stream. From O to P
the trail is slightly obscure. At P is a good view of Bear
Creek from 60 ft. above it. Between P and T-307 (formerly
FS20) Q the trail is close to the stream, scenic and unob-
structed.

Heading S from T-307, Bear Creek Trail starts 200yd W of
the T-307 bridge (Q,Map 18) over Bear Creek. Watch for a
utility line. A USFS parking lot for about 5 cars is found on
the N side of T307 10yd W of Bear Creek. Because there is no
car access to Bear Creek at its mouth, the portion of the trail
S of T-307 along Bear Creek is considered to be part of the
Clarion River Trail. See the description below.

CLARION RIVER TRAIL   9.3mi(15.0km)
SCEN: 1   DIFF: II   COND: 3
SKI-: S4   NOTE: B,M,2   ELEV: 1310/1290
MAPS: Hallton, Portland Mills, Carman, USFA(A), Map 18 in this
      Guide
TRAIL SEGMENTS:
 (1) Irwin Run (T-307) to Arroyo Bridge   3.5mi
 (2) Arroyo Bridge to Bear Creek mouth   4.6mi
 (3) Bear Creek Mouth to T-307   1.2mi

    In decades past, a chemical company along Spring Creek
near Hallton carried its wares to Portland Mills via a railroad
along the Clarion River. The chemical company is long gone,
but the old RR grade is still there--tree-shaded and pleasant,
with some outstanding scenic sections and excellent views of
the Clarion River. The first 2.5mi of RR grade upstream of
Hallton run through several summer home sites and hence is not
considered to be part of Clarion River Trail. The remainder of
the route to Portland Mills is almost entirely on public lands
(USFS and State Gamelands) and is ideal for day hikes.
    The best way to see the Clarion River is by canoe. You
should have prior experience at canoeing however, since minor
rapids and swift current can be challenging. If you don't own
a canoe you can rent one from any one of several canoe liveries
on the Clarion. These include:

Loves Canoe Rental, 3 Main Street,   Ridgway,   PA 15853
(814-776-6285)
Cook Forest Canoe Livery, P.O.Box 14, Cooksburg, PA 16217
(814-744-8094)
Forest View Canoe Rental, P.O.Box 105, Cooksburg, PA 16217
(814-744-8413)
Numerous river-side campsites are available for canoeists tak-
ing 2- or 3-day trips. The Clarion is usually too low in July
and August. Plan summer trips within a few days after a rain.
Access: To get to the downstream (W) trailhead, drive E from
Hallton along the N bank of the Clarion River for 2.5mi to a
public boat access at the mouth of Irwin Run Z (Map 18) where
Hallton-Laurel Mill Road (T-307) turns NE, away from the river.
A parking lot here is well-used by fishermen and canoeists. To
get to Arroyo Bridge, drive NE 1.4mi to an intersection. Turn
right (S) and drive 1.4mi to Arroyo Bridge (built in 1901) W.

Parking at Arroyo Bridge is available for a few cars near the S
end of the bridge (on the W side of the Clarion River). To get
to the E terminus of Clarion River Trail from the W terminus,
don't turn right at the above-mentioned intersection, but continue straight to the T-307 bridge over Bear Creek. Parking
for 4-5 cars is available in a fisherman's parking lot (Q ,Map
18) on the W side of Bear Creek on the N side of T-307.

Segment 1: The trail leading upstream (E) from the Irwin Run
parking lot Z is obvious. (The old RR grade also extends W
from the parking lot along the N side of the road toward Hallton and is hikeable for 1.mi to where it crosses to the S side
of the road and becomes a private driveway.) The first 2.0mi
of trail are exceptionally scenic. Drop off the trail at Y
to the river bank where a large rock offers a good view of the
Clarion. Embedded in a smaller rock to the left of the larger
rock is a 4" solid iron rod with an eye ring. These were probably used for raft launching, stopping and tie-ups during the
logging activities early in this century or late in the 19th
century. About 0.3mi further on is a grove of large hemlocks.
Some huge white pines are also to be seen along the trail. At
Cole Run are the remains of the old RR bridge (huge wood
columns, etc.) across Cole Run. You must find a small trail
down into Cole Run and up the far side to where the RR grade
resumes. Skirt a private property on the river side. From
here to Arroyo Bridge the trail becomes progressively more obscure and overgrown. Unless you enjoy exploring the ruins of
an early-20th-century tannery you may prefer to walk along the
dirt road a short distance uphill from the trail.

Segment 2: At Arroyo Bridge W the old RR grade trail continues E along the N side of the Clarion. For a nice lunch-stop
in the vicinity of Arroyo Bridge, seek the footpath leading
downstream between the S bank of the Clarion and a parallel
jeep trail. After 0.2mi drop down to the mouth X of the unnamed tributary of the Clarion via an obscure side trail in a
spruce woods.

From Arroyo Bridge W continue E and then N on the old RR
grade along the Clarion River. At the point where the Clarion
turns E again, the old RR grade vanished (crosses the river on
a long-gone bridge). From there follow a broad, dry terrace E
and then SE, slightly above the river level. The woods (hemlock, beech, pine) are so open that no trail is needed. At the
downstream end of an island V climb up to an open area covered with low-bush blueberry. Follow a discernable game trail
which follows the contour for 0.1mi. Angle downhill a short
distance and cross the four branches of a stream's delta U .
(A trail starting above the E bank of this stream takes you
well up the hill and then fades away, but an easy bushwhack N
will bring you out on T-307.)

Continue along the Clarion River to a second side stream
 S . (For a shorter hike, turn N and walk up this second valley to Hallton-Laurel Mill Road (T-307). About 0.6mi from the

Clarion River in southern Allegheny National Forest.   Photo by Carolyn Yartz.

Clarion are several meadows where this side trail becomes somewhat obscure. Use a compass to cross these open area to where
the trail reappears. Skirt several private homes along T-307
on the right.)

From the mouth of the second side stream, continue E
(upstream) on a pleasant trail along the Clarion River to near
the mouth of Bear Creek. Turn left (N) and walk 0.3mi to a
narrow woods road following a utility line corridor. Follow
this road 0.9mi N to T-307, 200yd W of the T-307 bridge over
Bear Creek ⬚Q.
NOTE: A scenic 4.6mi trail also runs E from Arroyo Bridge
along the S bank of the Clarion River as shown on Map 18. It
was in good condition in 1982, but was in poor condition (overgrown, fallen trees) in 1989. It is on Pa. State Gamelands.
There was once a bridge running E-W over the Clarion River at
⬚A. The trails on both sides of the river use the old RR
grade that once crossed this bridge.

IRWIN RUN TRAIL   6.1mi(9.8km)
SCEN: 2   DIFF: II   COND: B
SKI-: S4   NOTE: B,M,6   ELEV: 1750/1290
MAPS: Hallton, USFS(A), Maps 17, 18 and 20 in this Guide
TRAIL SEGMENTS:
  (1) Clarion River to FS136   3.1mi
  (2) FS136 to Lower Bear Creek Trail 3.0mi (est.)

From the parking lot (⬚Z,Map 18) that is the W end of
Clarion River Trail one can also walk N along scenic Irwin Run.
Remains of an old logging grade, plus open woods, provide easy
walking. The stream itself is the prime attraction. There are
remains of old log dams, probably dating back to logging days
early in this century. One can walk at least as far as the
Allegheny Plateau, a fairly level area full of grassy meadows
and old jeep trails joining long-abandoned oil- and gas well
sites. Map and compass are essential. Vegetation along Irwin
Run is mainly yellow birch, oak, maple, beech, hemlock, white
pine, rhododendron and larch.

The final two miles joining Irwin Run Trail to Lower Bear
Creek Trail have not yet been scouted. Eventually we would
like to scout a trail down Italian Shanty Run or Pole Road Run.
This will create a triangular loop trail for 3-day backpacking
trips (Bear Creek Trail, Clarion River Trail, Irwin Run Trail).
Allegheny Plateau's woods are open and full of old logging
trails and old logging RR grades. Italian Shanty Run and Pole
Road Run probably has jeep trails and/or old RR grades, so no
trouble should be anticipated (at least for those with topo
maps, a compass and the skills needed to use such tools).
Access: Parking is available along Hallton-Laurel Mill Road
(⬚Z,Map 18) in the lot between the road and the Clarion River.

On FS136, 2-3 cars can park just before the FS161 gate ($\boxed{\text{O}}$,Map 20)

Segment 1: At 0.7mi $\boxed{\text{B}}$ is a large white pine and the remains of an old rock-log dam. There is a 1980 clearcut (CC) at 1.6mi (Map 18). The trail crosses Irwin Run's stream bed several times. Don't get more than 20yd from the stream bed. At 1.9mi $\boxed{\text{D}}$ a pipeline crosses Irwin Run. Using the foot bridge, cross to the E bank and hike 0.1-0.2mi uphill. Explore just to the S of the pipeline to see the remains of the virgin timber of the 1920s. Recross the foot bridge to resume the Irwin Run hike. At 2.5mi ($\boxed{\text{N}}$,Map 20) is a stand of larch trees. Cross to the E bank of Irwin Run here and continue on to FS136 at 3.1mi $\boxed{\text{O}}$.

Segment 2: Continue N on FS136 for 0.1-0.2mi to FS161 (gated) leading NE. Follow FS161 (rarely used by vehicles) 0.8mi, passing a clearcut on the right, to $\boxed{\text{Q}}$ (Map 17). From here an old logging RR once traveled NE and branched, one branch going down Italian Shanty Run and the other going down Pole Run. The routes of these railroads (taken from an old railroad map) are shown on Map 17 as ooo. These potential routes to Lower Bear Creek Trail have not yet been scouted.

Notes for Explorers: The dirt jeep road just W of Irwin Run is gated at its S end. It is not interesting for walking. To make your trip into a loop hike by exploring the area W of Irwin Run on the return trip, the trails labeled (Y) (Map 18) are uninteresting. The trail labeled (Z) is nice because it goes through mature timber.

BIG RUN TRAIL   7.4mi(11.9km)

SCEN: 2	DIFF: II	COND: C
SKI-: S4	NOTE: B,M,6	ELEV: 1800/1330

MAPS: Hallton, Portland Mills, USFS(A), Maps 17 and 20 in this
      Guide

TRAIL SEGMENTS:
  (1) FS130 to Owls Nest (FS136)   5.7mi
  (2) Owls Nest to Bear Creek   1.7mi
      (Bear Creek to B.C. Picnic Area   0.8mi via U.B.C.Trail)

Big Run Trail runs from FS130 (N of Hallton, along Spring Creek) up Big Run to the Allegheny Plateau. It then follows gas-line swaths and jeep trails to Red Lick Run where it joins Upper Bear Creek Trail 0.8mi N of Bear Creek Picnic Area. Near the W end of the trail (State Game Commission land) the woods are mostly cherry (multi-trunked), aspen and maple. There are many open areas and you will probably see signs of bear. Most of the lower trail was an old RR grade. Early in this century logs from 20,000 acres of fcrest were hauled down Big Run to "Big Run Junction" (current location of the W trailhead) on their way to mills at Sheffield. Only 50% of the trail is on Forest Service land. The remainder is on State Gamelands (SGL#28) where camping is illegal. The description below refers to a number of stream crossings. However one also has the option of remaining on the N side of Big Run on a pleasant old RR grade the entire way.

Access: At the W trailhead ([A],Map 20) is State Gamelands parking for 20-30 cars just S of the FS130 bridge (wood deck) over Big Run on the W side of the road. (This bridge is still out as of 2/90.) (The dirt road slicing up the hill to the NE is gated by the Game Commission.) The jeep trail following the stream is also crudely gated. The E trailhead at Bear Creek Picnic Area offers ample parking. There is ample parking at Owls Nest.

Segment 1: Starting from the W, follow the old RR grade NE along Big Run. Up to [B] there are broad meadows with scrubby growth, but walking is pleasant. At [C] and [D] are old beaver dams dating back to 1982. (Beaver currently (1989) live nearer to the W trailhead.) At [E] rock-hop across Big Run. (Local lore calls this area "Hucklebone Curve".) The trail is now a narrow grassy lane right along Big Run. There is a large clearing above the trail here. The stream bed between [E] and [F] is solid, flat rock.

   At [F] the trail recrosses the creek. At [G] is a good campsite. At [H] is a nice stand of Aspen. Cross Big Run here. (One can also cross further upstream using a seldom-used gas-company-game-commission road ford. Two 4" gas lines also cross here, and these could be used to cross Big Run during high water periods.) Big Run Trail resumes 200yd upstream from this crossing. At [I] encounter 3 grades. Take the lowest one. Also at [I] is a metal-pipe foot bridge to the N bank of Big Run. (It will probably be removed in 1990.) At [J] the trail ceases to be passable. Cross to the N side of the stream to get onto the RR grade trail that takes you NE and then N. Upstream of [J] is an old beaver dam. An artesian well can be found by scouting around in the vicinity of [J]. At [K] turn ENE onto a gas-line swath. The swath is level, easy walking (good ski-touring). The swath soon turns N and, at [L], another pipeline corridor leads NE to Owl's Nest and FS136.

Segment 2: At Owls Nest is a large pumping station. Continue on along the gasline swath heading ENE. At [M] is a grove of Tamarack. Red Lick Run is encountered after 1.2mi. Follow it to Bear Creek. \Map 17\ Cross Red Lick Run near its mouth and then cross Bear Creek. You are now on Upper Bear Creek Trail, 0.8mi N of Bear Creek Picnic Area. See the description of Upper Bear Creek Trail on page 144.

Pigeon Run Falls along Pigeon Run Falls Trail. Photo by
Carolyn Yartz.

PIGEON RUN FALLS TRAIL   5.9mi(9.5km)
SCEN: 1   DIFF: II   COND: C
SKI-: S4   NOTE: B,M,?   ELEV: 1800/1366
MAPS: Hallton, USFS(A), Map 20 in this Guide
TRAIL SEGMENTS:
 (1) FS130 to FS136   5.9mi

     Pigeon Run Falls Trail passes the only natural water falls
in the SE sector of the ANF that we know of. It also passes
two other ponds, a nice change from stream-following. About
75% of the trail passes through State Gamelands No.28 (where no
camping is allowed). About 50% of the trail follows a narrow
stream valley. There are nice campsites at the W end of the
trail and at the falls. The trail should not be used in times
of high water because it crosses Pigeon Run many times.
Access: The W trailhead is 7.5mi E of Marienville on FS130,
[P] just beyond the bridge over Spring Creek. There is ample
parking. NOTE: The FS130 bridge at the mouth of Big Run was
washed out in June, 1989, so FS130 is gated at Little Run. The
bridge will probably be replaced in the future. It was still
out in Feb.1990. Parking is ample at the E trailhead (Owls
Nest, FS136). One could join Big Run Trail at Owls Nest.
Segment 1: Starting from the W (FS130), head N on an old RR
grade, crossing over the mouth of Hill Run. The trail follows
this obvious RR grade N along Spring Creek for 0.8mi to where
Pigeon Run enters Spring Creek [Q]. Turn right (E) here onto
another old RR grade where Pigeon Run enters Spring Creek. At
1.0mi an old logging road goes N across Pigeon Run at the State
Gamelands boundary. Just above this crossing is a nice rock
waterfalls, [R] known locally as Pigeon Run Falls.
     Continue ENE beyond the falls on the old RR grade. The
raised RR bed is easy to follow as it winds its way up the narrow valley, crossing Pigeon Run several times. Many apple
trees are found along this grade. At 2.7mi Pigeon Run intersects a large pipe line at BM1628. Jog right, then left to
find an old OGM road [S] going E up a grade. State Gamelands
signs are also seen near the OGM road. After reaching the top
of the grade, intersect another OGM road and continue E. Note
a pond to the right [T] (not shown on the topo). Just beyond a
road gate, turn left onto a woods road which takes you to the
large pond [U] shown on the topo. This pond has several large,
planted fields around it. Cross the breast work of the pond
and bear right on an access road. Follow this road 0.5mi and
turn left onto a pipeline just before the intersection with a
dirt road [V] that goes to Owls Nest. Follow the pipeline
0.4mi and cross the headwaters of Big Run [W] on an 8" pipe (or
hop across). Continue across the open meadows on the pipeline
swath 0.4mi to where you meet an OGM road [X]. Turn right (S)
and continue 0.4mi to the large clearing at Owls Nest [Y].

LAUREL MILL HIKING/SKI-TOURING TRAILS

11.0mi(17.7km)

SCEN: 2	DIFF: I	COND: A
SKI-: S1-S2	NOTE: M,0	ELEV: 1700/1400

MAPS: Portland Mills, USFS(A), Map 18 and 23 in this Guide
TRAIL SEGMENTS:
  (A variety of loop routes)

Some of these trails are groomed for ski-touring in the winter. Intersecting loops are well-signed. Trails are all blazed with blue diamond blazes. These trails provide an opportunity for hikes of a variety of lengths on even treadways. They are well-maintained. They pass through hardwoods, soft-woods and mountain laurel. Some trails S of T-307 are semi-primitive and provide an excellent opportunity for more vigorous hikes. They, also, are well blazed. The trail system is in the Ridgway Ranger District.

Access: Drive 3.0mi W of Ridgway on Laurel Mill Road (T-307). A large national forest sign is located at the entrance. Also, a large parking lot is seen on the N side of T-307. An information board shows the trails on a large wooden map. Brochures on the trail are also available. It may be advisable to ask the Ridgway Ranger District office (See page 25) to send you a brochure well in advance of the time you plan your visit.

Segments: See the detailed trail description on the brochure available at the trailhead or obtained from the Ridgway Ranger District.

BUZZARD SWAMP AREA
MAPS: Marienville East, USFS(A)

The Buzzard Swamp area is a 15 sq.mi tract of relatively isolated, gently rolling forest, interrupted by large marshes. Ironically, the area is named for John Buzzard, one of the loggers who nearly decimated the region early in the twentieth century. Located 4.mi E of Marienville on the road to Loleta, the area contains several large water impoundments, built and managed by the Pennsylvania Game Commission for propagation and hunting of waterfowl. Other areas are managed for the hunting of upland birds and game mammals. State Gameland and USFS roads surround the Swamp, making convenient access from the periphery. For interior access to the Swamp use FS157, a gravel road that begins at the large Buzzard Swamp sign on Marienville-Loleta Road and winds for 3.mi through second-growth hardwood forests, passing active beaver dams, marshes, and a few conifer plantings, before reaching a small parking lot at the management area. Occasional natural gas drill holes are relatively unobtrusive. Although game management is intense in the central portions of the Swamp, one need only hike or slosh away from the parking lot for a few minutes to lose sight of the signs of civilization. As one wanders through the

marshland, more beaver ponds are discovered. Deer lounge in
beds deep within dense willow thickets, and many species of
water birds may be seen. In wooded areas, one finds squirrels,
ruffed grouse, flocks of wild turkeys, black bear and bobcat.
     When visiting Buzzard Swamp, do not enter the signed
"Propagation Areas" where waterfowl can nest in seclusion. The
heavy hunting pressure every autumn must also be considered.
The Marienville East quadrangle topo seems to be quite accurate
and hikers may use the few foot trails or abandoned logging
roads depicted. Cross-country travel across the relatively
flat land will be hampered only by the marshes, where proper
safety precautions and care for the delicate environment must
be taken. Warm-weather footwear in the marshes may be as
extravagant as rubber hipboots or as simple as old tennis
shoes. Sturdy hiking boots suffice for forest travel. Cross
country skiing and snowshoeing are possible when the snow lies
deep over the frozen marshes.

BUZZARD SWAMP SKI-TOURING TRAILS   8.0mi(12.9km)
SCEN:. 2   DIFF: II   COND: A
SKI-: S1-S2   NOTE: M,?   ELEV: 1700/1600
MAPS: Marienville East, USFS(A), Map 22 in this Guide
TRAIL SEGMENTS:
  (1) FS376 to FS376   ?mi (several loops)
  (2) FS157 to FS157   ?mi (several loops)

     These loop trails are generally wide and flat. They are
well-signed at all intersections and are marked with blue diamond blazes. They could be used for hiking, but they were
designed mainly with ski-touring in mind. They are within the
scenic Buzzard Swamp Wildlife Management Area. No trail groom-
ing is provided. Motorized vehicles are not allowed beyond the
entrance parking area. Contact the Marienville Ranger District
(See page 25) for a description of the 8 or so loops in the
system.
Access: See Songbird Sojourn Interpretive Trail for information on the FS157 (S) access. For the FS376 (N) access, turn
onto FS130 at the center of Marienville (or onto the road that
passes between the Gulf station and the Bucktail Hotel). Drive
3mi E to FS376 which leads to the parking area.
Segments: See the Forest Service descriptions of these trails.

SONGBIRD SOJOURN INTERPRETIVE TRAIL   1.6mi(2.6km)
SCEN: 1   DIFF: II   COND: A
SKI-: S4   NOTE: M,I,0   ELEV: 1800/1700
MAPS: Marienville East, USFS(A), Map 22 in this Guide
TRAIL SEGMENTS:
 (1) FS157 to FS157 (loop)   1.6mi

    This interpretive trail has 26 interpretive sights which
are listed in pamphlets available at the trailhead. The blue-
blazed trail, itself, is not suited for camping or backpacking.
Plenty of camping opportunities are available in the vicinity
(Kelly Pines, Loleta Recreation Area, Beaver Meadows Campgrounds, Clear Creek State Park and Cook Forest State Park)
The trail intersects the Buzzard Swamp Ski-Touring Trails. It
is located in the Marienville Ranger District.
Access: Drive S from Marienville for 1.5mi on State Route
27027. Turn left onto FS157 and drive 2.5mi to the trailhead
on the N side of FS157 shortly before a gate across FS157.
Segment 1: The trail is easily followed without detailed
instructions.

LOLETA HIKING TRAIL   3.0mi(4.8km)
SCEN: 2   DIFF: II   COND: A
SKI-: S2   NOTE: M,1   ELEV: 1600/1300
MAPS: Marienville East, USFS(A), Map 22 in this Guide
TRAIL SEGMENTS:
 (1) Loleta Recreation Area to Loleta Rec. Area   3.0mi

    Loleta Hiking Trail is a loop trail used mainly by campers
at Loleta Recreation Area Campgrounds where the trail begins
and ends. It features a large rock overlook and surroundings
of a variety of mature timber.
Access: Loleta Recreation Area is 6mi S of Marienville via
State Route 27027, a blacktop road. Ample parking is available
in the main parking lot of Loleta Recreation Area. The trailhead is signed S of Sugar Camp Run.
Segment 1: Start by following an old RR grade E along Sugar
Camp Run. At [A] begin a gradual climb up the hillside to the
right, passing through some hardwood timber before swinging
back down to Sugar Camp Run for an easy rock-hop crossing [B].
The trail then passes several pine plantings as it gradually
climbs away from Sugar Camp Run Valley. After reaching the
ridge-top plateau [C] the trail swings SW through a mature timber stand. At [D] is a large rock overlook surrounded by mountain laurel and rhododendron. The terrain becomes rockier and
the footing less secure. Eventually the trail slopes down toward the E Branch of Millstone Creek, and runs parallel to it
on the E side before turning [E] to return to the Group Campsite #2 road. From there it is a short walk back to the parking lot in the Recreation Area.

Tornado damage in the Tionesta Scenic Area--Cherry Run.   Photo by Carolyn Yartz.

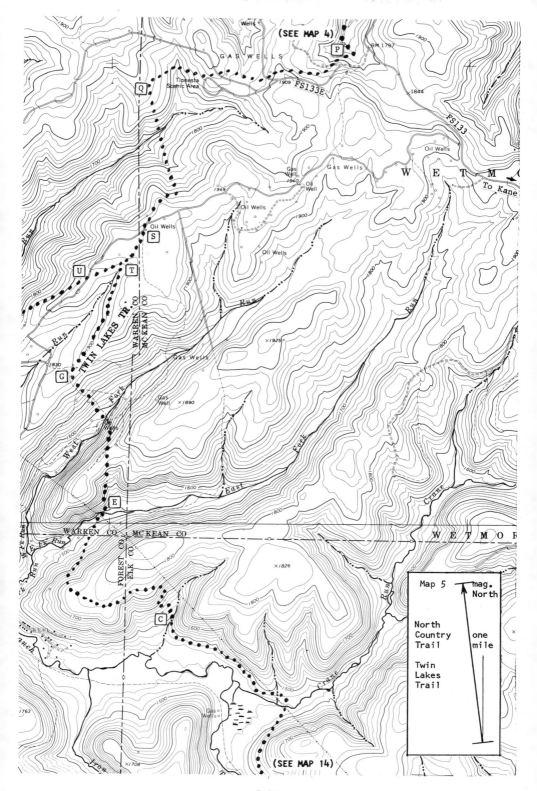

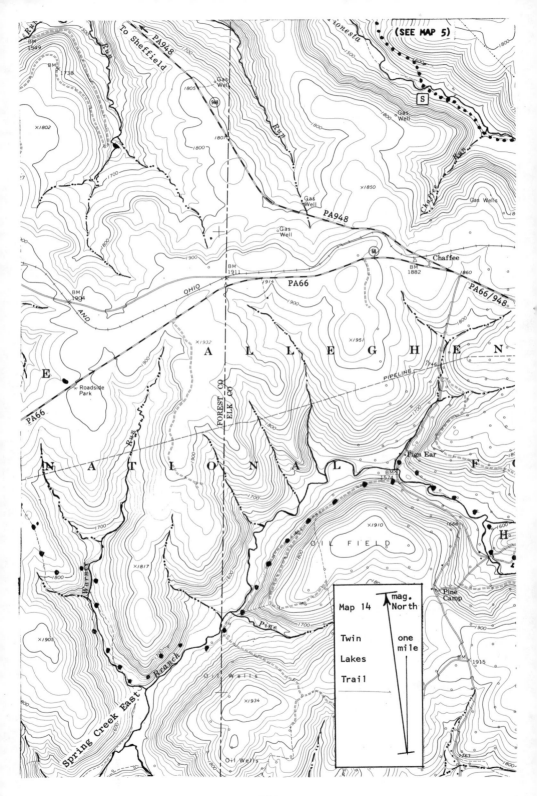

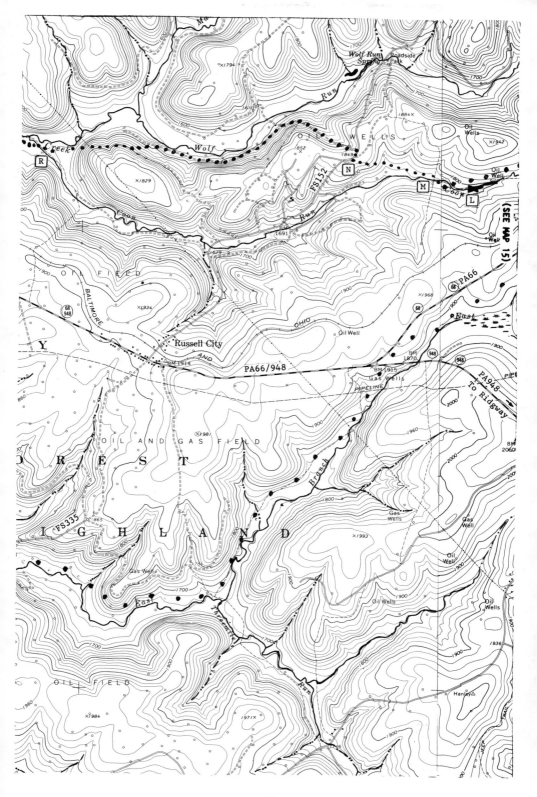

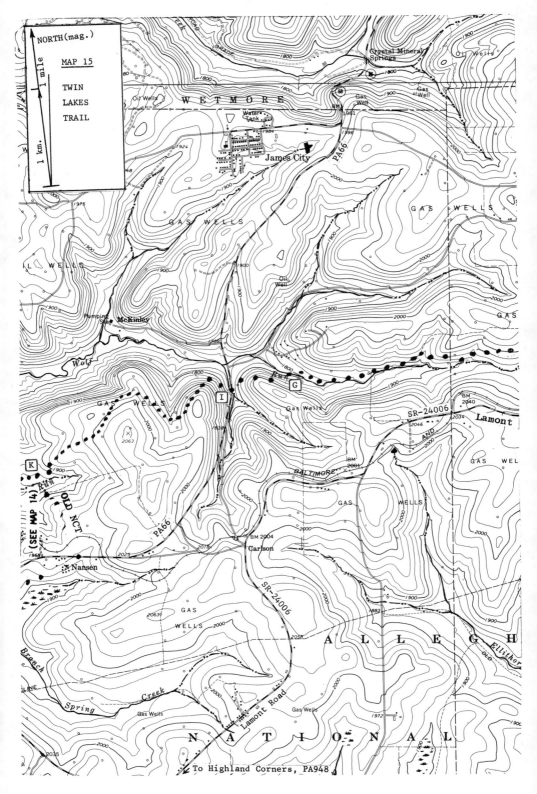

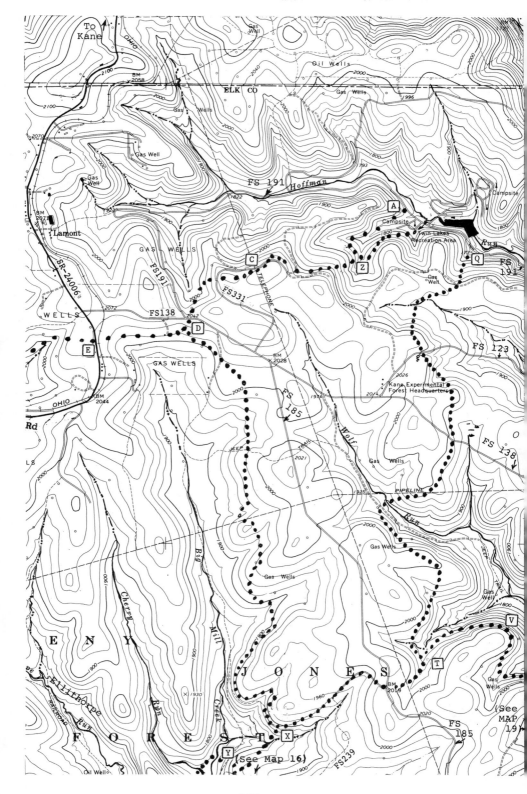

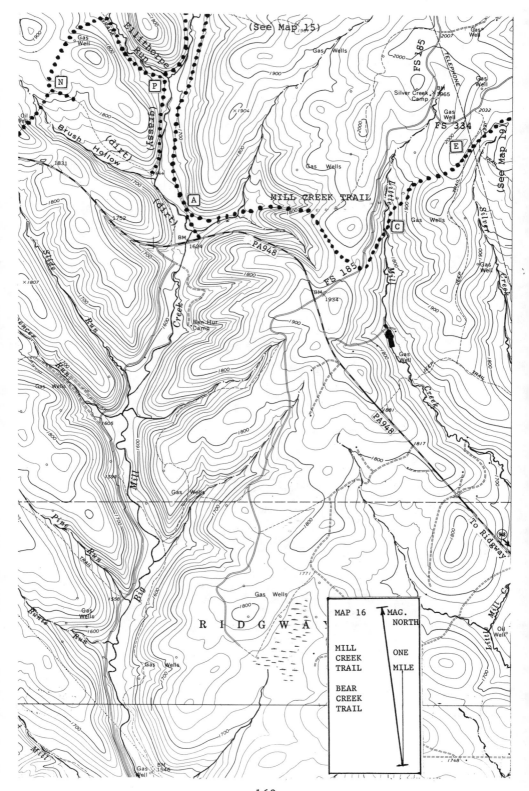

Cable bridge over Wolf Run on Twin Lakes Trail. NOTE: The USFS
is removing bridges that oil-and-gas people no longer maintain
Photo by Fred Feit.

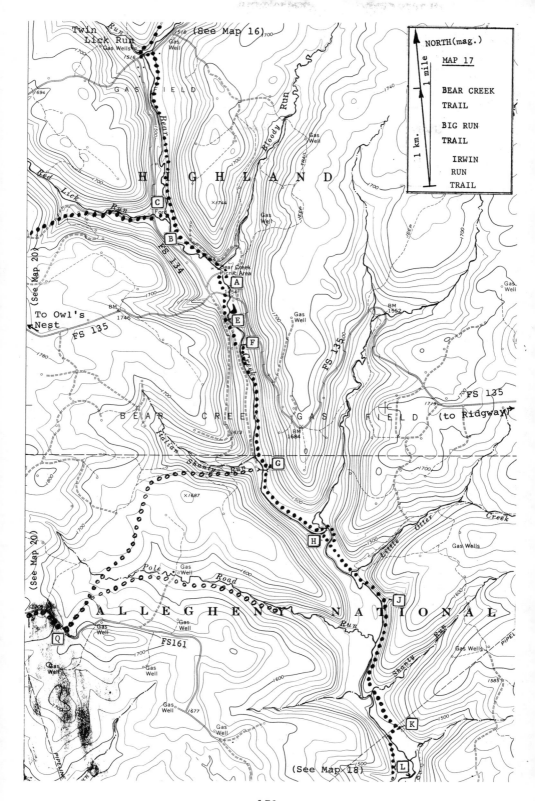

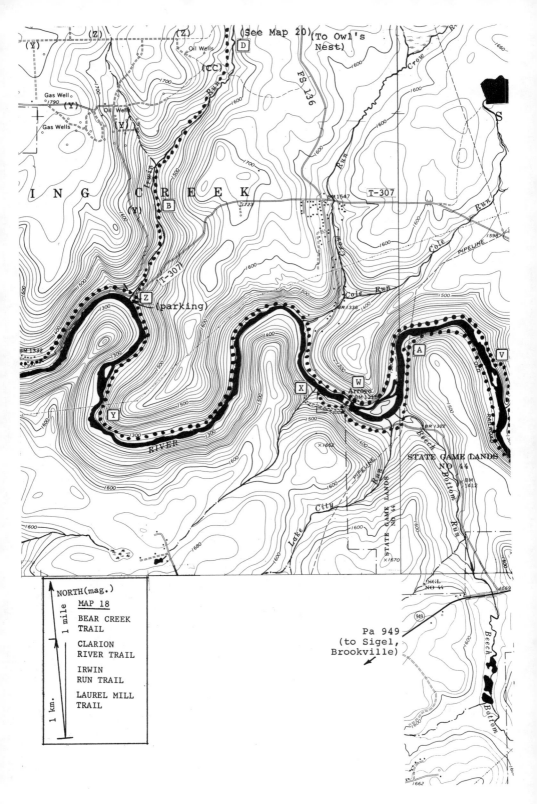

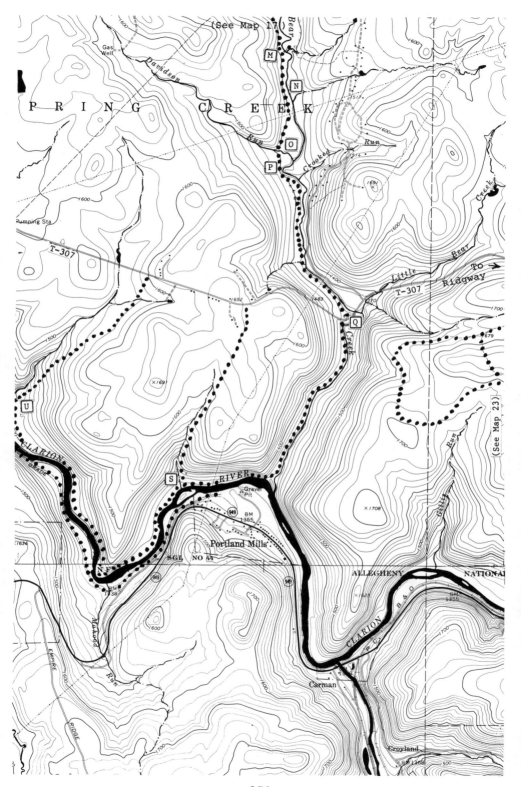

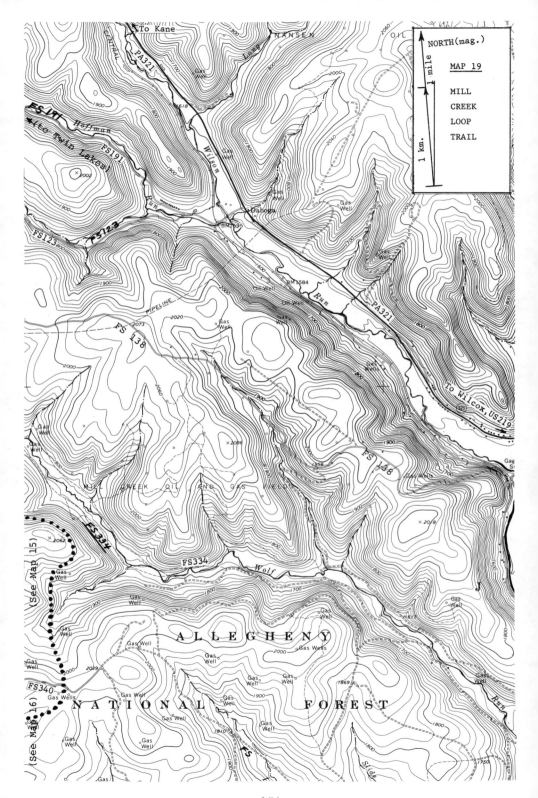

Allegheny National Forest is full of little make-shift bridges.
This two-cable model across Bear Creek is one of the more
challenging ones. NOTE: The USFS is removing bridges that oil-
and gas people don't maintain. Photo by Bruce Sundquist.

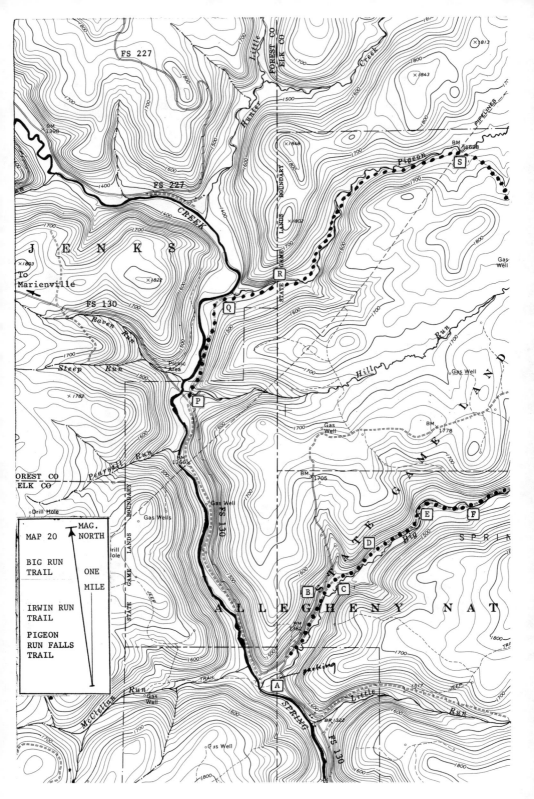

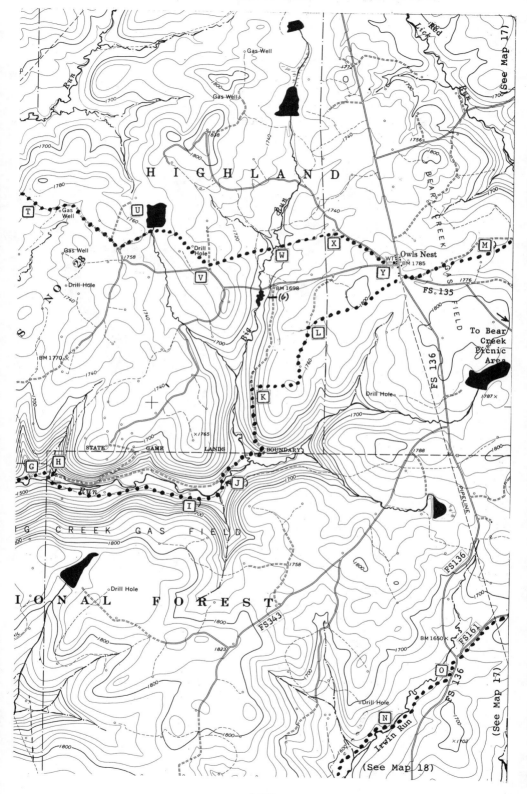

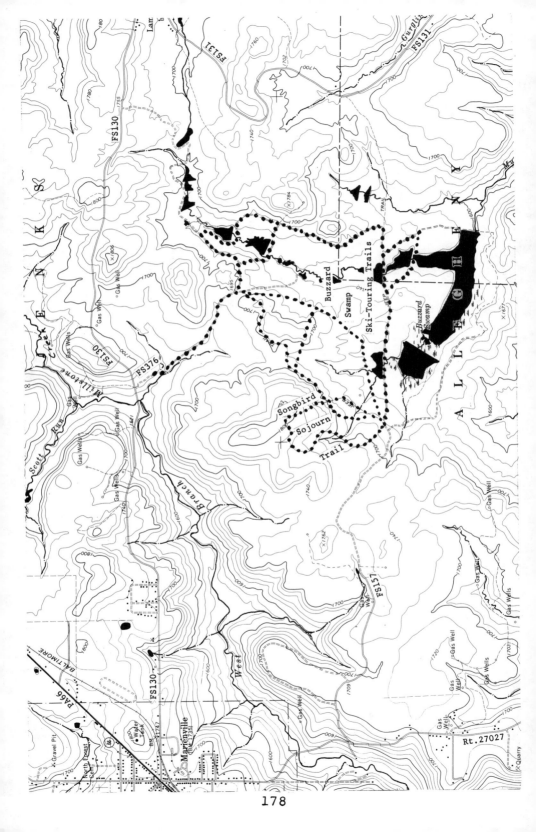

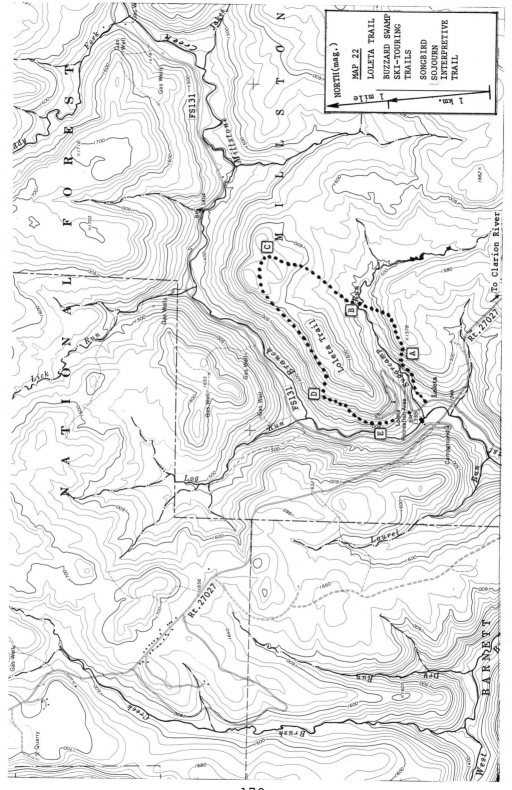

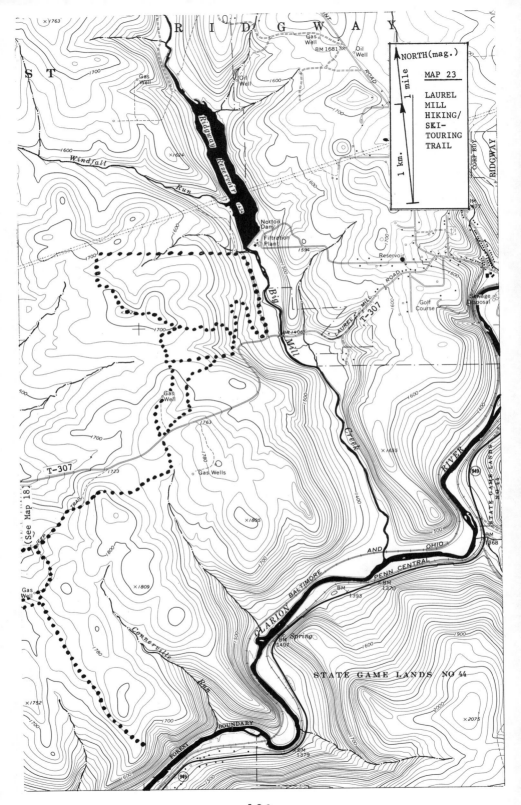

APPENDIX I: ABOUT THE SIERRA CLUB

The Sierra Club was founded in California in 1872. It has long been recognized as one of the nation's most active national groups working for environmental integrity through public education, lobbying, and legal action. The national membership is about 500,000. The Pennsylvania Chapter's membership is over 20,000. In recent years the Sierra Club has focussed its environmental advocacy on clean air and water, open space and wild places, conservation of natural resources, wise use of land, and improved mass transportation.

The Pennsylvania Chapter has worked on the abuses of strip mining, returnable-beverage-container legislation, flood-plain legislation, oil- and gas drilling regulations, environmental education, wetlands protection, limiting off-road vehicle use in Allegheny National Forest, opposing construction of a pump storage generating facility in St. Anthony's Wilderness (Dauphin County), opposing Philadelphia's plans for increased sewage discharges into the Delaware River, protecting Pennsylvania's north-central mountain scenery, and other issues.

The Pennsylvania Chapter maintains a lobbying office in Harrisburg to work on state legislative issues. This office is the only full-time environmental lobby in Harrisburg.

For more information regarding Sierra Club activities or membership information, contact any of the following groups.

Allegheny Group,   Lake Erie Group   Headwaters Group
P.O. Box 8241   P.O. Box 332   1019 Granger Dr.
Pittsburgh, PA 15217   Edinboro, PA 16412   Johnstown, PA 15905

If you live in Ohio, contact the state chapter, 145 N. High Street, Columbus, OH 43215 (614-461-0734) for the address of the Sierra Club Group nearest to you.

If you live in New York, contact the state Chapter, 234 Hudson Ave. Albany, NY 12210 (518-472-1534) for the address of the Sierra Club Group nearest to you.

Besides environmental advocacy in the political arena, the Sierra Club has a number of programs aimed at broadening the base of public commitment to the conservation ethic. These include:

Outings

The Club sponsors about 300 trips yearly, both national and international, for people of all ages and skill levels. A few of the dozen or so trip categories are: base-camp, canoe-kayak, backpacking, ski-touring, river rafting, cleanup. Most local groups sponsor weekend outings.

Sierra Club Foundation

This non-political arm of the Sierra Club receives tax-deductible contributions for such purposes as research (forestry, wildlife, wilderness-impact, etc.), sponsoring conferences, producing films, books and other educational material, purchasing land, paying for public-interest lawsuits, etc.

Legal Defense Fund

About a dozen full-time attorneys plus dozens of volunteer, part-time, public-spirited attorneys make up this arm of the Sierra Club. They work to obtain compliance with the letter and spirit of federal and state environmental laws. Many cases of national significance have been won.

Publications

Numerous outstanding publications on environmental matters are produced by the Sierra Club. These include professional-quality films, slide shows, photographic essays, National News Reports (a weekly summary of conservation news and related legislative activity, available for $15/year), the Sierra (the monthly newsletter of the Sierra Club), soft-cover books, and group- and chapter newsletters. The Pennsylvania Chapter's newsletter, the Sylvanian comes out six times per year and reports on the activities of all ten or so local Sierra Club groups in Pennsylvania. In addition, some local groups also have their own newsletters.

Allegheny Group

The Allegheny Group holds monthly meetings on the second Wednesday evening of each month in the Pittsburgh Garden Center behind the Scaife Unit of the Arts and Crafts Center, Fifth and Shady, starting at 7:30 p.m. Call their recorded message at 561-0203 to learn what the next program is to be about and to learn about forth-coming outings. Group outings (mainly hiking and ski-touring, with some backpacking, bird-watching, nature walks, cycling and canoeing) are held nearly every weekend throughout the year. Outings are listed in the Sylvanian. An attempt is made to accomodate all skill levels. Non-members are welcome on Group outings. The only cost involved for a trip is the car-pool fee (3.5 cents per passenger mile). Members may also become involved in various conservation committees that work on such issues as air quality, oil and gas issues, wetlands, recycling and political education. Besides publishing the Allegheny National Forest Hiking Guide, the group also publishes the Hiking Guide to Laurel Highlands Trail (along the top of Laurel Ridge). Annual membership fees are $33 (1990) which includes membership in the Pennsylvania Chapter and the National Sierra Club.

The Allegheny National Forest was once the home of giants.
This stump is along the Laurel Mill Trail. Photo by Carolyn
Yartz.

Other Outdoor Groups that Visit Allegheny National Forest

Allegheny Outdoor Club

This informal group of outdoor enthusiasts is involved mainly in hiking and ski-touring. Their trips are usually within the Allegheny National Forest and vicinity and usually on Sunday afternoons. An annual membership fee of $1.50 per person covers the cost of mailing their outing schedules. Their outing schedules are also published in the Warren Times-Observer. Hikes are normally not scheduled during December, July or August. Membership is about 50, and typical trip attendance is 10-15 people. The Club maintains 26 miles of the North Country Trail--from Tionesta Scenic Area west to Dunham Siding. To learn more about the AOC, contact Marjorie Neel, President, Star Route, Sheffield, PA 16347 (814-968-5415).

American Youth Hostels, Pittsburgh Council

This group meets nearly every Thursday evening at 8:30 at their headquarters building behind the Arts and Crafts Center, Fifth and Shady. Their activities include hiking, backpacking, ski-touring, cycling, canoeing (flat-water and white-water), kayaking (white-water and lake), rafting, climbing, and caving. The group has its own canoes, cycles, rafts, kayaks, climbing gear, etc. which it rents to members on their outings. It's not unusual to have 6-8 outings on a weekend. Typical trip attendance is around 10 people but some trips attract over 100 people. The group sponsors schools in white-water canoeing, climbing, kayaking, ski-touring, etc. for a broad range of skill levels. They also publish guides to hiking and canoeing in Western Pennsylvania, plus an "AYH Outdoor Food Book". They also maintain the Baker Trail which extends from Freeport to Allegheny National Forest. For more information, contact AYH at 6300 Fifth Avenue, Pittsburgh, PA 15232, 412-362-8181. Annual membership dues range from $10 (Junior) to $30 (Family). This includes a monthly newsletter. Non-members can go on AYH trips by paying an additional $2 fee per trip-day. The normal trip fee is 50 cents per day.

INDEX

TRAIL NOTES